Economical with the Truth

Economical with the Truth: The Law and the Media in a Democratic Society

Edited by

Dimity Kingsford-Smith B.A., LL.B (Syd.) LL.M (Lond.)
Solicitor, Supreme Court, New South Wales
Lecturer in International Comparative Law
University College London

Dawn Oliver M.A. (Cantab.)
Barrister, Lecturer in Law, University College London

ESC Publishing Limited
Oxford
1990

Published by
ESC Publishing Limited
Mill Street
Oxford OX2 0JU
United Kingdom

ISBN 0 906214 59 9

Typeset by Advance Typesetting Limited, Oxfordshire
Printed by Information Press Limited, Oxford, England

Contents

Foreword

The threats to freedom of speech in Britain are serious and they are increasing. Unlike most democratic countries, our constitutional and legal system does not guarantee the basic right to communicate and receive information and opinions, subject only to necessary exceptions. From a legal perspective, freedom of speech, British-style, is what is left to us by the constraints of statute law and common law. In other words, the right to public communication is merely the residuary legatee, after the claims have been met of the rapidly spreading common law of contempt of court, of confidentiality, and of personal privacy, of the old and unreformed law of defamation, and of the streamlined and enforceable new criminal legislation on official secrets. Unlike many modern democracies, Britain still lacks a freedom of information law with a right of public access to government information. Unlike many modern democracies, Britain also lacks statutory protection against unwarranted invasions of privacy.

The new-fangled common law on contempt and confidential information is enforced by the courts without the safeguard of trial by jury (a safeguard regarded by Dicey as essential and worth a hundred constitutional guarantees of free speech). In the aftermath of the *Spycatcher* litigation, it is all too easy for powerful groups (including public authorities) to prevent free speech by obtaining wide-ranging interlocutory injunctions, binding on third parties through the new contempt doctrine.

Libel apart, Blackstone's celebrated disapproval of prior restraints on publication is regarded by English judges as radical American nonsense. Government arguments for suppressing speech, worthy of King George the Third's Ministers, prevail in the Queen's Courts.

The broadcasting media are subject to a statutory regime which involves extensive regulation, self-censorship, government interference, and even direct state censorship. The Peacock Committee rightly observed that the end of all censorship arrangements would be a sign that broadcasting has come of age, like printing three centuries ago. Yet, for all its stated support for a genuinely free market in broadcasting, the Government shows no sign of abandoning state regulation and control. We may well have the worst of both worlds: the destruction of public service broadcasting and the retention of unnecessary state interference.

Time and again, Article 10 of the European Convention on Human Rights has had to be invoked as a substitute for a positive guarantee of free speech in this country. Traditionally, in the English legal system, since the right to free speech has no enforceable constitutional protection, the starting point is the property or other interests of the person seeking to prevent expression, and the newspaper or journalist has the task of persuading the court that proprietary or other rights or interests should exceptionally be displaced or overridden.

The European Convention approach is very different. The starting point is the right to impart and to receive information and opinions. That basic right may be interfered with only if the aim of the interference is legitimate and if the means of achieving the aim is reasonably proportionate to meet a pressing social need. It was upon that basis that the European Court of Human Rights held that the House of Lords had breached Article 10 in imposing a contempt injunction on the *Sunday Times*, in the *Thalidomide* affair. It was upon that basis that the European Court would have been likely (but for the Government's wise tactical surrender) to have ruled that the Law Lords had breached Article 10 in finding Harriet Harman guilty of contempt for giving a journalist confidential documents obtained on discovery but read out in open court.

One central question now raised before the English courts in three pending appeals is whether our Judges will interpret and apply Article 10 to protect free speech in the Strasbourg way, even though Article 10 (like the rest of the Convention) has still not been incorporated into English law. One case challenges the blanket ban imposed by the General Medical Council on advertising by medical practitioners; a second case disputes the post-*Spycatcher* contempt doctrine, as applied to newspapers; the third case attacks the Sinn Fein broadcasting ban as disproportionate to the Government's aims.

In the *Spycatcher* litigation, several judges seemed willing not only to refer to Article 10 but also to take it seriously. The decisions in these three subsequent cases show a marked reluctance to use the 'pressing social need' test, with its principle of proportionality, as the touchstone where free speech is at stake.

The entire range of interlocking subjects, covered by 'information law', continues to be bedevilled by the failure of successive governments to introduce comprehensive legislative reforms. During the past 15 years, seven official committees have reported on various aspects of information law. Some of these reports are being implemented; others still gather dust on departmental shelves. What is wholly lacking is a coherent public policy about information and expression, notably the unifying principle that whoever needs information for any legitimate purpose should be able to obtain the information unless there is some clear, specific and compelling reason for it to be withheld.

The subject-matter of this book is therefore important and topical, and its publication is well-timed as a contribution to an important debate. The comparisons with the United States (by Anthony Lewis) and with France (by Roger Errera) are particularly illuminating for British readers. It is to be hoped that these essays will be influential in increasing freedom of expression and ending unnecessary state controls, whether by Parliament, the Executive, or the Judiciary.

Anthony Lester Q.C.
Temple
London

Preface

The *Spycatcher* affair has highlighted how precarious is the freedom that the media enjoy in Britain. The *Jeffrey Archer* case has brought home to the public that the press can and does from time to time abuse its freedom. It is therefore timely to give consideration to the role of the media in a democracy, and to consider the various rationales that are advanced from time to time in favour of press freedom, or in favour of restrictions on that freedom. How may the press be protected in performing its proper democratic functions, and yet be restrained from abusing its very considerable powers?

In any society the press performs a range of functions. It disseminates information and ideas and it influences opinion, on political, religious, aesthetic, moral and other matters. It acts as a channel of communication between the members of the community and state and other institutions. In a sense it is the market for ideas and information, and looked at in this way it is surprising that a government dedicated to the operation of a free market should have challenged the press repeatedly in the last ten years.

In countries where the press is not free from state control it serves to propagate state policy, to mould public opinion in conformity with the wishes of the state and to protect the state from criticism and embarrassment. In societies where the press is free from state control the reverse is often true – the press can and does criticise the state, propagate alternative policies and criticise and embarrass the powerful. The present Government supports not only a free economy, but also a strong state, and here lies an explanation for its attacks on press freedom when it is seen to undermine the authority of government.

The relationship between state institutions and the press is inherently problematic and conflictual. Governments need the press to promote their image and policies, but they resent adverse press comment and the dissemination of information that lays them open to criticism. The press often needs the co-operation of government if it is to have access to the opinions of ministers.

The last decade has seen a sharp decline in the relationship between the Government and the press. The Thatcher Government, bent on transforming society, the economy and popular attitudes, and on building a strong central state, has taken an intolerant, authoritarian-partisan approach to much press reporting. There has been a succession of confrontations between government and the press – the *Zircon* affair, *Spycatcher*, 'My Country Right or Wrong', the Gibraltar shooting, the banning of interviews with IRA sympathisers, the Harrods takeover report. On some occasions, it has to be admitted, the press have acted irresponsibly and brought calumny upon themselves, particularly in reporting scandalous and often inaccurate matters to do with the private lives of public figures.

These issues are not of course purely parochial; in this collection we have brought together perspectives from the United Kingdom, the United States and France; the perspectives of journalists, academic and practising lawyers, historians and, vicariously, of one of our greatest philosophers, Jeremy Bentham; and the perspectives of the late eighteenth and nineteenth centuries as well as those of the late twentieth century.

In the first essay Anthony Lewis provides an American perspective on some of the problem areas of press freedom. His article 'Journalists and the First Amendment' is based on the 1987 John Foster Memorial Lecture. He considers that the true rationale for press freedom is to enable the public to assert meaningful control over the political process. He compares the ways in which the United States Supreme Court deals with questions concerning the freedom of the press with the unprincipled, pragmatic English approach which does not promote public control over politicians. This reflects the different cultural traditions of the United States and the United Kingdom, but he suggests that the case for a Bill of Rights protecting, *inter alia*, press freedom, is strong. Freedom of the press is not, he acknowledges, without disadvantages, especially when the press encroaches on personal privacy; the press is entitled to freedom because of the evil it prevents, rather than on account of the good that it does.

The next three essays home in directly on the *Spycatcher* affair and the issues it raises for journalists and freedom of the press. David Pannick, who was counsel for a number of the newspapers involved in the various *Spycatcher* cases, gives an account of the history of that litigation. He suggests that English judges did not appreciate the rationales for free speech as provided, for example, in Article 10 of the European Convention on Human Rights to which this country is a party (although the Convention does not form part of our law). Nevertheless there is a need for a workable set of laws to protect truly sensitive information concerning national security, and he suggests that this should be met through administrative measures and co-operation with our allies rather than by futile attempts to suppress information through court injunctions.

A government bent on suppressing information has a number of legal techniques at its disposal; prosecution under the Official Secrets Act 1911 or, when it comes into force, the 1989 Act, is one. But prosecution carries risks, as the *Ponting* case showed. The burden of proof is high in criminal proceedings, and juries are notoriously reluctant to convict where the information disclosed does no harm to the public interest. Further, prosecution takes place after disclosure, often when it is too late.

Civil law in the United Kingdom, unlike the USA with its First Amendment, offers the possibility of prior restraint on publication via interim injunctions against publication where, *inter alia*, a breach of confidence is alleged. In civil proceedings the burden of proof is lighter and there are no juries. Hence the Government chose to take civil proceedings for breach of confidence in order to stop publication of *Spycatcher*.

But the question arises whether the private law of confidence is an appropriate method of preventing publication of official secrets. In the third essay Rodney Austin suggests that it is inappropriate to use the law of confidence, designed to protect commercial secrets and those of private relationships, to protect information in the name of the public interest, as government has sought to do repeatedly in the last 15 years. He suggests that a new statutory framework is required to deal with these cases; and the security services need to be subjected to effective independent scrutiny.

The readiness of governments to attempt to suppress the publication of sensitive or embarrassing information makes the freedom of speech of Members of Parliament even more important as a means of exposing inefficiency or iniquity; yet the political impact of the right of Members of Parliament to free speech will be reduced if the goings on in the Houses of Parliament cannot be relayed to the public by the media. This issue of the freedom of the press to report on Parliament – even a right on the part of Parliament to be reported – was one of the side issues in the *Spycatcher* litigation, and it arose again in the Harrods takeover affair in April 1989. This topic is discussed in the fourth essay in this collection 'Parliament and the Press'. It is argued that Parliament's increasing concern to be reported in the media indicates a fear that it will be bypassed and its influence undermined, and communication between government and the public will take place directly through the press to the exclusion of Parliament unless Parliament can 'get in on the media act'.

Much of the political function of the media is performed by broadcasters, who are regulated in their political coverage to a far greater degree than the press. Broadcasting media differ from the press in that the air waves are a limited resource and hence their use has to be regulated or rationed. Nor can broadcasting be easily financed by viewers in the same way that newspapers can be financed, to some extent at least, by readers. Licence fees are difficult to collect and hence much of the financing for radio and television broadcasting must come from advertisers. Alan Boyle in 'Do Broadcasters Need Free Speech?' considers what is currently happening to and being proposed for the future of broadcasting, and its effect on political coverage.

The British tradition has been of public service broadcasting, but this is currently moving towards a 'free speech – free market' orientation. The background to this change, he suggests, is partly political: the Government's dislike of the evenhandedness of BBC and IBA coverage of politically controversial issues. But it also reflects an ideology of competition and the free market. The changes however could mean that there will be little or no coverage of political issues, or else very one-sided (*Sun*-sided?) coverage. The USA experience of television coverage of political issues is not an encouraging example, and the prospects of the future of broadcasting in the United Kingdom, in this respect at least, are uncertain. Alan Boyle suggests that continuing regulation of programme content alone can secure the provision of high standards of public service broadcasting.

The fifth essay in the collection makes comparisons on a range of freedom of speech issues between French and English law. It has been natural in the past to look to the United States and the other common law jurisdictions for points of comparison in English law; but our membership of the EC and strengthening of links with mainland Europe will surely draw our legal system towards the European civil law tradition. M Roger Errera, Conseiller at the Conseil d'Etat in France, points to the constitutional protection for 'freedom of communication' which gives the press in France extensive protection against state imposed restrictions. The right is not, however, unconditional. French law recognises a right to privacy which has so far been absent from English law, though attempts were being made in 1989 to secure the passage of a private member's bill creating a right to privacy to overcome the excesses of the press in cases like the *Jeffrey Archer* libel suit.

In France state secrets are protected by a variety of measures not so very different from the English law. If *Spycatcher* had happened in France, however, it is doubtful whether the French Government would have instituted proceedings against the author and publishers in foreign courts, or sought to prosecute or take disciplinary proceedings against a retired civil servant.

M Errera also looks at French and English law on the *sub judice* rule and other measures to protect the integrity of trials, the law relating to disclosure of a journalist's sources (discussed in Andrew Lewis's paper in this collection), *Zircon* affair style searches of journalists' offices, and other restrictions on publication of immoral or blasphemous material. He concludes that the United Kingdom Government seems to be more willing than the French Government to resort to the courts to prevent publication, but that it might be that the rights of individuals are better protected in some respects in the United Kingdom than in France.

The last two papers examine the Utilitarian approach to the general problem of press freedom and the particular question whether journalists should be required to disclose their sources. This latter issue was topical in the *Spycatcher* case and in other recent litigation. Philip Schofield and Andrew Lewis are both engaged on the Bentham Project at University College London and they discuss Jeremy Bentham's writings on these issues. Bentham's Utilitarian approach provides an illuminating perspective to the role of the press in a democracy and to the protection of journalists' and others' sources.

The *Independent* case of 1985 to 1986 raised the question of the intellectual foundation of the privilege professionally claimed by journalists not to reveal their sources. The issue in this case was whether a journalist could and should be required to disclose his sources, for example where, as in this case, he had discovered and disclosed information on a matter into which the Monopolies and Mergers Commission were inquiring. The Commission took the view that access to the journalist's sources was necessary for the purposes of their investigation.

The judge at first instance found the journalist, Jeremy Warner of *The Independent*, to have a reasonable excuse for refusing to disclose his sources, namely 'the public interest in the protection of journalists' sources'. The Court of Appeal and the House of Lords took the opposite view and ordered Jeremy Warner to make the disclosure. He refused and was fined £20,000.

Given that there are a number of arguments in favour of and against the final result of the case, how are we to judge the judges' decision in this matter? Andrew Lewis applies Jeremy Bentham's theory of evidence to the question in his paper on 'Bentham's View of Journalists' Privilege and the *Independent* Case'. Bentham's views on privilege from disclosure (not of journalists for they did not exist as a recognised profession in Bentham's day) of priests receiving confessions and lawyers receiving communications from their clients, proceeded from the basis that the burden is on the person arguing for exclusion of evidence to establish that the vexation, delay and expense caused by disclosure outweighs the arguments in favour. The arguments in favour of disclosure are strong – the rooting out of iniquity and taking of legal proceedings to deal with it to protect the public. The arguments against disclosure on grounds of vexation, delay and expense are less strong, and the journalist's case is not entirely persuasive. Andrew Lewis suggests tentatively that Bentham, applying these criteria, would have favoured a law requiring journalists to reveal their sources. Whether the Utilitarian approach is the most appropriate one is a matter for debate.

Finally, Philip Schofield considers the role of the press in a democracy according to Bentham's Utilitarian theory. For Bentham the press was an organ of the 'Public Opinion Tribunal' – the public generally – and in this role the press was an essential part of the democratic process. It plays a part in combating 'political corruption' and securing the promotion of the interests of the whole people as opposed to those of the ruling class.

Bentham identified two ways in which a government might seek to prevent publication of material that it found objectionable – prosecution and licensing. Prosecution, he felt, would be unattractive to governments, and licensing would be preferred. Rodney Austin's article illustrates how perceptive Bentham was on this point. Yet Bentham was not an unreserved supporter of the press, and he expressed concern about invasions of privacy by the press interfering with the happiness of individuals.

In the light of the *Ponting* case, *Spycatcher*, the reform of the Official Secrets Act and current concern over privacy, Bentham's discussion of the role of the press and the relative attractions of criminal and civil law restrictions on publication could not be more topical and more penetrating, despite the lapse of years since he was writing.

Dimity Kingsford-Smith
Dawn Oliver
University College London
September 1989

Journalists and the First Amendment

Anthony Lewis

The Public Right of Free Speech

My subject is the role of free expression in our kind of political society. I come to it as a journalist, and freedom of the press is in issue today in both Britain and the United States. There are tensions between the press and the Government, the press and the law. But my purpose here is not to argue the rights of the press. It is to argue the rights of the public: in Lord Scarman's words, 'The public right of free speech'. Let me begin by indicating why I believe the question should be defined in that way.

Martin Chuzzlewit, in the Dickens novel, crosses the Atlantic in a packet boat. When it reaches New York, newsboys come aboard shouting out the latest in their papers: *The New York Sewer*, the *Stabber*, the *Plunderer* and so on. 'Here's the *Sewer*'s exposure of the Washington gang,' one cries, 'and the *Sewer*'s exclusive account of a flagrant act of dishonesty committed by the Secretary of State when he was 8 years old, now communicated, at a great expense, by his own nurse.'

No one but Dickens could make the point with such extravagant gusto. But others felt a distaste for our press then, and do now. How self-righteous it can be, and how outrageous. Today Americans would add: how powerful. Our papers no longer have to retail fancies of the crimes committed by political leaders in childhood. We have a press that exposes real official wrongs: a press that helped to force a President from office and pushed candidates out of the 1988 campaign for the White House.

That kind of press arouses resentment: hardly a surprise. 'The press is the enemy,' President Nixon instructed his staff. Politicians less prickly than he have felt victimised by the press. And resentment does not come only from the victims. Among the public, too, there is a feeling that the press has grown arrogant in its power. 'Who elected you?' people ask. The question echoes Stanley Baldwin's complaint that the press lords of his day wanted 'power without responsibility'.

Anthony Lewis B.A. (Harvard), Lecturer in Law, Harvard Law School, Columnist for the New York Times

Why should a self-appointed group of people have the power to root about in our national life, exposing what they deem ripe for exposure? The American press would say the Constitution of the United States answered that question. The Framers made the choice when they put in the First Amendment the command: 'Congress shall make no law . . . abridging the freedom of speech, or of the press.'

Those are sweeping words. But the First Amendment is not what some in my profession assume it is: a declaration that the press must always prevail in any legal contest, that journalists are a preferred class. The purpose of the clause assuring the freedom of the press was not to serve the interest of editors and publishers. It was to serve the interest of society. So the great cases teach.

This is not an essay about American law, I assure you. But I am going to give an anecdotal account of three decisions of our Supreme Court. I do so to make a point that is not parochial. Even in a country whose fundamental law explicitly protects the freedom of the press, that freedom is seen in a larger social and political framework.

On 29 March, 1960 *The New York Times* carried an advertisement with the heading 'Heed Their Rising Voices'. It was what we call message advertising, seeking support for the civil rights movement in the South and in particular for Dr Martin Luther King Jr. The text deplored what the police and other elements of the then dominant white segregationist forces in the South had done to peaceful protestors against racial discrimination. It said that Dr King had been arrested seven times and his home bombed, that black students in Montgomery, Alabama, had been expelled after singing a patriotic song, 'My Country, 'Tis of Thee', on the steps of the state capital.

The advertisment named no names among the forces it criticised. But a commissioner of the city of Montgomery, Mr L. B. Sullivan, claimed that it would be taken as reflecting on him because he was in charge of the local police. He brought an action for libel, seeking $500,000 in damages. *The Times* could not offer the defence of truth, because it found that the advertisement was inaccurate in some particulars. Dr King had been arrested four times, for example, not seven; and the students had sung not 'My Country, 'Tis of Thee' but 'The Star-Spangled Banner'. At trial in Alabama the judge found the advertisement 'libellous per se'. He instructed the jury to bring in a verdict for Mr Sullivan if it found that the advertisement was 'of and concerning' him. It did, awarding him all he had asked, $500,000.

Four other Alabama politicians brought libel actions over the advertisement. They sought $3 million in damages, and there was every reason to expect juries to award that amount in total. *The Times*, then a marginally profitable newspaper, was at risk of survival. Moreover, other libel actions were brought against *The Times*, broadcast networks and national magazines over news reports on the South. It was plain that the hallowed common law action for libel was being used for a new purpose – a political purpose, to frighten national news organisations out of covering the racial struggle.

It is only 25 years ago, but we can hardly remember conditions in the American South then. Blacks were barred by law – law that had been found unconstitutional but was still enforced – from attending schools with whites or entering most hotels or eating at lunch counters. In large parts of the South blacks were kept from voting by intimidation and trick and murder. It may indicate the atmosphere if I tell you that *The New York Times* had great difficulty in finding a lawyer in Alabama who would represent the paper in the *Sullivan* case. When one did agree to take the case, and he invited *The Times*'s New York lawyer down to discuss it, he booked the visitor into a motel 40 miles away under an assumed name.

Would it have mattered if the national press had been scared off by those libel actions and had stopped paying close attention to the racial conflict? I think it would have made a great difference.

Most Americans were not aware of the cruel reality of racism until the news reports of the 1950s and 1960s confronted them with it. Professor Alexander Bickel of the Yale Law School wrote that television coverage of mob resistance to school desegregation brought concretely home to viewers what the abstract idea of racial segregation meant. 'Here were grown men and women,' he said, 'furiously confronting their enemy: two, three, a half dozen scrubbed, starched, scared and incredibly brave colored children. The moral bankruptcy, the shame of the thing was evident.'

Americans reacted politically to what they saw and read. Congress passed laws that utterly changed the South, so that blacks now vote freely and hold political office – and it is a region that looks to the future instead of the past. It was an astonishing social change, and it happened in part because the press performed its function.

The press was able to keep covering the civil rights movement because the Supreme Court set aside the libel judgment for Mr Sullivan. That may sound easy to do: a huge sum, awarded to a man not mentioned in an advertisement because of trivial errors in the text. But the Supreme Court has no power to review the decisions of state courts on matters of state law. It can only correct them when they run foul of the Federal Constitution. And libel had always been considered a matter for state law. In 170 years the First Amendment had never been held to apply to libel cases.

Counsel for *The Times* in the Supreme Court, Professor Herbert Wechsler of the Columbia Law School, met that challenge of history by calling on history himself. He reminded the court that long ago, in 1798, Congress had passed a Sedition Act making it a crime to publish false criticism of the Government or its leaders – and that James Madison, the principal author of the First Amendment, had condemned the Act. It was a violation, he said, not only of the freedom of speech and press but of the whole premise of our new Constitution: that the people were to make the ultimate political judgements. Madison said the Sedition Act threatened 'the right of freely examining public characters and measures, and of free communication among the people thereon, which has ever been justly deemed the only effectual

guardian of every other right'. Professor Wechsler relied on that early statement of the centrality of free political speech in a free society. He said this libel
action suppressed the freedom as effectively as a direct prohibition on speech
or publication about the racial issue. 'This is not a time,' he told the court
'– there never is a time – when it would serve the values enshrined in the
Constitution to force the press to curtail its attention to the tensest issues that
confront the country.'

The Supreme Court agreed. In an opinion by Justice Brennan, it held that
the First Amendment allowed robust and uninhibited speech about political
life, including even unpleasantly sharp attacks on those in office, and that
inadvertent mistakes in such political criticism could not be the basis of libel
judgments.

The American press celebrates the case of *New York Times v Sullivan* as its
greatest legal victory in modern times. But it was not a press case in the narrow
sense. The crux of Justice Brennan's opinion is in a passage noting that, under
our law, officials are broadly immune from libel actions for what they say in
the course of their duties, the purpose being to encourage vigour in their
performance. 'Analogous considerations,' Justice Brennan said, 'support the
privilege for the citizen-critic of government. It is as much his duty to criticise
as it is the official's duty to administer.' The passage expressed James
Madison's view. The object of the Constitution is to preserve public control
over the men and measures of government. The press is protected not for
its own sake but to enable a free political system to operate. In the end
the concern is not for the reporter or the editor but for the citizen-critic of
government.

The *Sullivan* case demonstrates, I think, what is at stake so many of the
times when we speak about freedom of the press. It is the freedom to perform
a function on behalf of the polity. Nowadays, Justice Powell of our Supreme
Court has said, 'no individual can obtain for himself the information needed
for the intelligent discharge of his political responsibilities . . . By enabling
the public to assert meaningful control over the political process, the press
performs a crucial function in effecting the societal purpose of the First
Amendment.'

Now let me go back several decades, to a case decided by the Supreme
Court in 1931: *Near v Minnesota*. Near was the publisher of a weekly
newspaper that made crude attacks on public officials, accusing them of
corrupt alliances with gangsters. The paper was also viciously anti-Semitic. In
1925 the Minnesota legislature passed a law allowing the courts to close,
as a public nuisance, any newspaper found to be persistently malicious,
scandalous and defamatory. Local authorities brought an action to enjoin
further publication of Near's paper, and the Minnesota courts did so.

That was almost the end of the case. Establishment newspapers were
embarrassed by Near and reluctant to argue the principles of press freedom on
his behalf. But eventually they did support an appeal to the Supreme Court.

By a vote of five to four, the court found that the Minnesota law violated the First Amendment.

Chief Justice Hughes, who wrote the opinion, devoted much of it to a discussion of English legal history: the struggle against licensing of the press, and Blackstone's conclusion that the liberty of the press meant putting no previous restraints on publication. But then Hughes turned to James Madison's words about the need for open public discussion to prevent abuse of official power. The importance of the press's function in that regard had grown, Hughes said. 'The administration of government has become more complex,' he said, 'the opportunities for malfeasance and corruption have multiplied,' and all that emphasised 'the primary need of a vigilant and courageous press'.

Great principles of law are often evoked by unworthy parties, and Near and his newspaper surely seemed to fall into that category. But a few years ago someone I know was working on a book about the *Near* case. He mentioned this in the hearing of Irving Shapiro, an American industrialist who was the chairman of the DuPont Company, and Mr Shapiro said: 'I knew Mr Near.' Irving Shapiro's father owned a small dry-cleaning shop in Minneapolis. Gangsters demanded protection money from him, and when he would not pay they sprayed the clothes in the store with sulphuric acid. No regular newspaper covered the event. But Near's weekly did, angrily and accurately. For all of Near's anti-Semitism, for all his excesses, he endeared himself to the Shapiro family – and made a difference in that community.

Forty years after the *Near* decision its principle that the First Amendment disfavours what we now call prior restraints was applied in a case not of local sensationalism but national security. It was the *Pentagon Papers* case. *The New York Times*, and later other newspapers, published excerpts from a secret official history of the Vietnam War. The war was still on, and the Government claimed that continued publication would gravely injure national security, threatening alliances and the lives of our soldiers. The Government went to court and asked for injunctions.

The judge chosen to try the case, Murray Gurfein, had been a military intelligence officer during the war – a fact that did not encourage *The Times*'s lawyers. He began with expressions of concern for the national security. But when he asked the official witnesses to point to particular passages in the secret history – the volumes were piled up before him in the closed courtroom – and tell him what harm publication would do, they were evasive. Judge Gurfein remarked at one point that he could see more sensitive material on the war 'every day on television'. After hearing the arguments he rejected the Government's application for an injunction. He said the Government had shown no threat of vital breaches in security but only the possibility of embarrassment. He sympathised with the difficulties of governing in such circumstances. But, he said, 'a cantankerous press, an obstinate press, a ubiquitous press must be suffered by those in authority in order to preserve the even greater values of freedom of expression and the right of the people to know.'

When the case reached the Supreme Court, the Court rejected the Government's arguments and allowed the newspapers to resume publishing the *Pentagon Papers*. Two legal doctrines played a part in the decision, and it is important to identify both.

First there was the principle of the *Near* case, that prior restraints are suspect under the First Amendment. Second was the absence of any statute directing the courts to prohibit the publication of such materials. Government counsel conceded that there was no Act of Congress defining this material as secret and calling for its suppression – as there is, for example, on nuclear information. The Government was asking the justices to make public law to fit the occasion, and they were reluctant to do that. If new law was needed, the Executive should go to Congress.

The Times counsel in the *Pentagon Papers* case was the late Professor Bickel, a man of conservative outlook who rejected the notion of absolute freedom, for the press or anyone else. At the end of the case he wrote that the First Amendment gave us no pat formula but rather ordained 'an unruly contest between the press, whose office is freedom of information and whose ambition is joined to that office, and government, whose need is often the privacy of decision-making'. When government lost control of information, he said, that was ordinarily the end of the matter: courts would resist the role of censor. Society would be better off if both parties in the contest exercised restraint, but we must be content with 'an untidy accommodation'. 'It is the contest,' he said, 'that serves the interest of society as a whole.'

Those are the three American cases I wished to describe. It may be necessary to add a footnote. Our constitutional law seems to strike some who see it from across the Atlantic as a strange creature, full of politics, not law in the old-fashioned sense. I put it to you that the judges and lawyers in the United Kingdom would find the judgments in those three cases entirely familiar in their reasoning process. Yes, the Supreme Court can be the subject of political debate, as it is now. But in their work the judges act very much as common law judges, reasoning from case to case, respecting precedent, preserving the sacred quality of the law. The Court is closely divided at times, but I suppose that is not unknown in the courts of last resort of other countries. And almost invariably, over time, the sharpest conflict yields to the development of legal doctrine that commands general assent. Justices of all views are moved by institutional loyalty and discipline. That was so in the Hughes Court, the Warren Court, the Burger Court – and it will be in the Rehnquist Court. I mentioned that *Near v Minnesota* was the first five-to-four decision. Just five years later a unanimous court applied its teachings in holding invalid a special tax on newspapers. One of the dissenters in the *Near* case, now speaking for the Court, said: 'Informed public opinion is the most potent of all restraints upon misgovernment.'

There Can Be No Accountability in the Dark

That statement returns me to the reason for bringing up the American cases. In them one can see a number of themes meaningful for any free political system, republic or monarchy, with or without a written constitution.

The first theme is society's interest in protecting freedom of expression. We value the freedom in part because of its liberating effect on the individual spirit; to forbid the poet or painter to express what he or she feels is to impose a form of imprisonment. But more and more we are concerned with the social function of free speech and a free press: to assure that, in a political system intended to be responsive to the public will, public opinion is informed. In a word, the purpose is accountability. Government must be accountable for what it does. And there can be no accountability in the dark.

The press and the citizen-critic of government need freedom to speak not only as a negative check, to prevent corruption or abuse of power. We believe affirmatively that better policy will emerge when there is a choice among possibilities. Wisdom is more likely to come from open debate.

A testament to that principle has come lately from an unlikely source: the Soviet Union. A writer and editor, Anatolii Ivanovich Strelyanyi, was talking to a meeting of young Communists at Moscow State University, and a transcript was made. He spoke of the need for a truly independent press.

'An independent press is a press that reports on killed and wounded in Afghanistan,' he said, 'gives daily information on radioactivity at Chernobyl, is present at sessions of the Politburo and reports on who said what.'

A voice from the floor said: 'That can't be.' Mr Strelyanyi replied: 'If we want to eat our own bread, not American bread, then there will be an independent press.' He went on: 'If there had been an independent press, then Medvedev, the chief engineer who 10 years ago wrote that you shouldn't build a nuclear reactor near Kiev and described the catastrophe . . . But they didn't let him have his say, they shut him up. And discussion was necessary.'

The Soviet Union, with its blundering economy, is a telling example of the cost of an unfree press and speech. We can look to another troubled society, South Africa, for an example of another theme that I see in those three American cases. That is that the crucial test of freedom today is not freedom to express opinion but freedom to argue facts.

It is often said that South Africa has a free press. The Government says so, and points to it as evidence that South Africa adheres to Western values. It is true that South African newspapers can criticise apartheid and make negative comments on Government policy. They are free, that is, to express critical opinions. But they are not free, not by any means, to publish inconvenient facts.

Even before the current emergency, a web of laws inhibited publication of facts crucial to an understanding of reality in South Africa. One made it a crime to print anything about prisons without first obtaining assurance of the story's accuracy – a requirement that the courts said amounted to seeking the prior approval of prison authorities. Another law imposed the same requirement for articles about the police. Military matters were another forbidden zone.

I do not need to say that what the army, the police and the prisons do is an extremely important aspect of the way the black majority lives in South Africa, and the way it feels. Most whites are entirely unaware of those realities; they have never entered a black township, for example. All of us tend to turn our eyes away from unpleasant truths about our own societies, but the unawareness of South African whites is extreme. And the Government is determined to keep them unaware. That way it is easier to convince them that unrest in the black community is the work of outside agitators and Communists. It is easier to maintain the maximum of repression with the minimum of guilt.

The emergency regulations have had an even more drastic effect in limiting current knowledge of the brutalities of daily life in the black townships. The authorities set out to do in far more severe form what Mr Sullivan and the others wanted to do in the American South: keep outsiders from knowing about the oppression. But the South African Government has largely succeeded. It has shown that international policy-making can also be affected by a cut-off of information.

When we look at South Africa, we have no trouble seeing that freedom of comment is not enough. But in any society informed policy choices require knowledge of the facts: facts about Soviet casualties in Afghanistan or the origins of the war in Vietnam. When he decided to let publication of the *Pentagon Papers* go ahead, Judge Gurfein said: 'In this case there has been no attempt by the Government . . . to stifle criticism. Yet in the last analysis it is not merely the opinion of the editorial writer or the columnist which is protected by the First Amendment. It is the free flow of information so that the public will be informed about the Government and its actions.'

The *Pentagon Papers* case illustrates a third point. It is that the fear of what may happen if there is open discussion of public issues is often exaggerated. When the Government was trying to stop publication of the Vietnam history, its witnesses appeared in closed sessions of the court and told Judge Gurfein that terrible damage would be done if publication went ahead. Years later one of those witnesses said in a public statement that he was glad the Government had lost the *Pentagon Papers* case. The things he worried about then did not really matter, he said – the supposed embarrassment with allies and so on. The affirmation of our freedom was more important.

The Case for the First Amendment

The fourth and final point that I see in these cases is the special danger of courts suppressing information at the behest of governments without the guidance of statute law. It is one thing for courts to build the law from case to case in areas untouched by statute, as Common Law judges always have done; it is quite another for courts to reshape the law to a design proposed by the executive when the legislature has acted in the field and has not made law to that design.

In the *Pentagon Papers* case, for example, the United States Government asked the Supreme Court to do what Congress had declined to do. Successive Administrations had proposed legislation to declare certain kinds of information secret and have courts enforce the rule by injunction. But Congress had not passed the bills.

We need have no illusions about the perfection of legislatures. They can legislate in haste and repent at leisure, as Congress did in the Espionage Act and Parliament in the Official Secrets Act. But ordinarily legislative consideration allows for canvassing of opinion in ways not open to courts, and for weighing of policy considerations. When rules are laid down by statute, they have a degree of democratic validation. Professor Bickel put it: 'The more fundamental the issue, the nearer it is to principle, the more important it is that it be decided in the first instance by the legislature.'

Moreover, there is an inherent imbalance in the parties when a court considers whether to prohibit speech or publication without guidelines in a statute. On one side there is the Crown or the United States, with all the weight of a government. On the other is a private individual or institution – a newspaper, say. Judges are trained to pay equal regard to parties, whatever their status, and I greatly respect their ability to do so. But when a newspaper asserts what it claims to be a general public interest in certain information, may there not be a degree of scepticism – a sense that there is really a selfish interest in publication? It is sometimes hard to see that such selfish interests are what add up to general freedom. Or consider the matter of national security. When a government contends that publication of this or that will endanger the nation, judges tend to be impressed; certainly American judges do. They are reluctant, quite naturally, to disagree with an official estimate of danger in an area – defence, intelligence and the like – in which judges are not expert. What chance does the other party have to persuade a court that there is no substantial risk, or none that outweighs the damage to freedom, when the risks have not previously been balanced by the legislature? In the United States, Congress has been reluctant to grant new powers to suppress information. That is the reason that Presidents have increasingly asked courts to act in the absence of legislation. But it is the very reason that courts should take care before making new law.

Freedom of the Press in the United Kingdom

Those are the themes that I see in the American cases of freedom of the press: the societal function of the freedom, the importance of allowing discussion of facts, the tendency to exaggerate the harm disclosure may do and the special danger of judicial law-making to limit free expression without legislative guidance. I said earlier that I thought they were meaningful considerations for any free political system. Let me try now to apply them in the British context. I do so uneasily. But it is necessary to exercise the freedom to disagree.

Consider first the case of the *Crossman Diaries*. Richard Crossman kept the diaries while a member of the Cabinet, as his colleagues were aware. After his death they were edited, a first volume was prepared for publication and serialisation began in *The Sunday Times*. The Crown brought a civil proceeding to restrain further publication. It chose not to invoke the Official Secrets Act, although that sweeping statute seemed on its face to apply. Why did the lawyers for the Crown make that choice? We can imagine some reasons. The Official Secrets Act had been much criticised. A jury might be reluctant to convict under it, especially when there was no claim that the diaries disclosed defence or foreign affairs secrets. It might be awkward to put in the dock as criminal defendants Mr Crossman's literary executors – among them his widow and Mr Michael Foot – and the editor of *The Sunday Times*. An order restraining publication could be issued with so much less inconvenience: by a judge alone, without a jury, and without the machinery of the criminal law.

The Lord Chief Justice decided not to stop publication because, he said, the disclosures were insufficiently serious. But he held that the courts had power to issue such a restraint, and the significance of the *Crossman Diaries* case lay in the fashioning of that legal instrument to curb expression on public matters. The Lord Chief Justice followed the legal path suggested by the Attorney-General. He applied in the public sphere the common law doctrine that condemns breaches of confidence in commercial and private relationships. His judgment took that large step without really considering the alternatives in public law that were open to the Crown. The judgment gave no weight to the fact that the Official Secrets Act existed and could have been invoked. Nor did it mention that governments had long been on notice of Mr Crossman's intention to publish and could have brought in a bill to deal with the problem – if one existed. In my view those were essential considerations. If Parliament has enacted law whose use the Crown finds awkward, it is not for courts to provide an easier way – least of all when freedom of expression is involved. In a free society repression of speech and press should not be made easy.

An even more extreme example of inadequate attention to the public interest, in my view, was the *Thalidomide* case. The interest was great: the need to discuss and correct flaws in the rules of drug testing that had allowed on the market a drug that caused horrifying birth defects. While tort actions by the affected families lay on the docket for a decade, with no move for trial, Parliament was prevented from discussing the problem by the *sub judice* rule. When *The Sunday Times* wrote about the situation, its articles were found by the House of Lords to be in contempt of court because they might put pressure on the defendant in the tort actions, the Distillers Company. And a final article, using company documents and charging serious faults in the promotion of thalidomide after questions had been raised about its effects, was also restrained as a violation of confidence.

The result of the *Thalidomide* case was to keep the press and the public from discussing the facts in a way that might help the victims of thalidomide and prevent another drug tragedy. Or that was the result until the European Court of Human Rights found that the suppression of *The Sunday Times* articles violated the European Convention's guarantee of freedom of expression. Then, as you know, the Government proposed and Parliament enacted a statute bringing the law of contempt into conformity with the European decision.

The Government avoided another defeat in the European Court like Byron's Julia, by a timely surrender. That was the *Harman* case, in which it was held to be a contempt to give a journalist copies of official documents, obtained in litigation, that had been read out in open court. I confess that I find myself unable to understand the logic of that decision. What legitimate legal or social purpose can be served by punishing the disclosure of something already disclosed? The Crown offered no answer when the case was taken to the European Court. It settled the case by paying costs and undertaking to change the law.

Finally there is *Spycatcher*. You would not expect me to forego mention of that controversy.

When the House of Lords initially forbade the publication of material from Peter Wright's book, even though it was a best seller in the United States and could be brought freely into Britain, there came to mind a film scene from my childhood. It was in *Mutiny on the Bounty*, starring Charles Laughton as Captain Bligh. Bligh orders a member of the crew to be given a hundred lashes for some offence. After 60 or so, a mate comes to him and says the man is dead. 'I ordered 100 lashes,' Laughton says, 'and it will be 100.' Pour encourager les autres, I suppose. That must be the logic. But it was obsessive in Captain Bligh, and I think it must be in the law.

The Press and National Security

The serious question raised in the *Spycatcher* case and others like it, the difficult question, is how a free society should deal with disclosures of intelligence matters. I have read *Spycatcher*, and there are things in it that I do not think should have been published. Some of the disclosures are on the disappointing side. We are told, for example, that agents with great industry and daring wired the French embassy in London and thereby discovered that General de Gaulle was opposed to Britain's entry into the Common Market.

But there are details of what is called tradecraft that should not have been disclosed – if they had not in fact been published earlier, in books to which the Government made no objection.

The work of the security services is necessarily secret. It would be easy to say that nothing should ever be written about them: easy but wrong. So the American experience indicates. For a long time the Central Intelligence Agency was out of bounds – never discussed in the press except in reverent generalities. Then, in 1974, a newspaper report (by Seymour Hersh in *The New York Times*) charged that the CIA had carried out a massive and illegal programme of spying inside the United States, tapping the telephones and opening the mail of thousands of innocent citizens. President Ford appointed a commission under Vice-President Rockefeller to study the charges. It found that the domestic illegalities had indeed occurred, on an even larger scale. Then a Senate committee that studied the agency reported that there had been attempted assassinations of foreign leaders, among them Fidel Castro. The consequences of those assassination attempts may have been grave; we cannot be certain yet what harm they may have brought back on us.

The lesson drawn was that even the highly secret work of intelligence needs accountability: a requirement to explain actions outside the agency, where self-interest and self-protection may inevitably cloud judgment. Corrective measures were taken to assure accountability. Intelligence agencies were required by law to report to special committees of the two houses of Congress. They have done so faithfully, with one or two damaging exceptions. And there have been no significant leaks of intelligence information from the committees.

It is sometimes argued that discussion of the intelligence services will harm their reputation. One of the majority judgments in the House of Lords in the *Spycatcher* case put it: 'The British public will lose confidence in the Security Services.' My impression is that the real injuries to public confidence in both our countries have come from faults in the services' performance – faults that could hardly remain unknown, such as the failed Bay of Pigs invasion or the Kim Philby affair. Disclosure and correction of such folly as the programme of domestic surveillance surely contributed to the political health of the CIA and the country.

A further point has to be made about the intelligence services, at least in the United States. What they undertake in secret sometimes reflects an important change in national policy, and such changes require public scrutiny. When US intelligence officials direct a secret war on another country, when they mine that country's harbours, American interests may be profoundly affected – and Congress and the public are entitled to debate the policy. Our recent history reinforces that claim. Policies undertaken in secret have had disastrous results. I need mention only one example: the covert transfer of arms to Iran. That was one of the exceptional occasions on which the legal obligation to report to Congress was violated. If the rules had been obeyed, I believe much damage would have been avoided.

The Cultural Dimension

In this as in this whole discussion there is a cultural difference between our two countries that has to be faced. Americans are given to noisy, open discussion of public issues. The British prefer decision-making in small groups, closely controlled. But it is not cultural bias that makes me believe Britain should and will move to a greater degree of public scrutiny, of open accountability. It is a sense that British society has changed, and is changing, in ways that make the old idea of policy discussion as the responsibility of a restricted group ineffectual and unacceptable.

Britain is a less homogeneous country than it was. There is a strong interest in giving all sections of the society the feeling that they have a share in its governance. You have a Prime Minister who has had extraordinary success in a stance of opposing the politics of deference and tradition. And, like all of us, you have television. Seeing what that medium has done to American Presidential politics, I cannot be enthusiastic about it. But it is a fact of life, and by all signs an irresistible one. It draws political leaders into a relationship with the viewing audience – the public at large – rather than with a small governing circle.

There is another difference between us that has to be recognised. The public right of free speech is not a prime value in this country. Judges often speak of it as a treasured right, but the results of case after case are to the contrary. Freedom to argue the facts of public policy loses out to the claims of confidentiality, foreign policy, legal order and so on. Even the most direct assault on press freedom seems to evoke little outrage. If American police ransacked the offices of a major broadcasting network, seizing vast amounts of tapes and documents, I do not think the responsible official would remain in office long.

Law seems to me to have a curious effect on the press in Britain. It discourages journalism that matters: the difficult work of digging into public issues. Looking at the decided cases, an editor would know that he is likely to meet great resistance and high cost if his paper tries to find out what caused a drug disaster. He will have no trouble if it prints stories under such headlines as 'Sex Boys for Sale at Queen's Grocers'. Of course the law is not wholly responsible, but I think it has played a part in the visible degradation of British journalism. Evelyn Waugh is beginning to look like a master of understatement. The popular press has gone, someone said, from gutter to sewer. Even the more serious papers, most of them, act as if their duty to freedom were fulfilled by critical comment. There are encouraging exceptions. But too many cover political life largely as transmission belts for unexamined assertions by politicians.

In such circumstances the profession can hardly gain respect. It must be difficult for those who want to work seriously as journalists to persuade sources of information – in government, business, science, wherever – to take them seriously. That is another price of a system that discourages coverage of the important processes in society and encourages the publication of fantasy and innuendo.

The great theatrical portrayal of journalists hardened to sensationalism and lies happens to have been an American play, '*The Front Page*', done superbly at the Old Vic years ago. The American press used to be filled with the vices I have just charged to Fleet Street, including – in the big establishment papers – the habit of 'cozying up' to politicians. Through the post-war years, until the mid-1960s, the Washington press corps was very easy on those in office. A symbiotic relationship, some have called it. That has mostly ended, for a number of reasons. The assumption on our part that government officials have superior knowledge and wisdom was shattered by Vietnam. Television let the public in on the little world of Washington. And, not least, our law – the law of the Constitution – encouraged a more vigorous exercise of the freedom of the press. That was what the three decisions I mentioned meant to journalism as a profession. They treated the press seriously, as an instrument of freedom and public accountability. It is not too romantic to believe that the press has tried to live up to that role.

That brings me to a last difference in our two societies: the written Constitution that we have and you do not, with all that it means in judicial enforcement of rights. There are deep historical reasons for the difference. 'We the people' – the opening words of our Constitution – created the United States with a government of limited powers. The people were sovereign. It followed almost inevitably that their compact would be binding on those who from time to time governed them. In Britain law-making power has never been attributed to the people. Parliament won that power for itself, and it remains the sovereign legislator.

But one does not have to be a great iconoclast to know that in practice today the power of Parliament is in good part myth. The Executive dominates the legislative process. Even with its select committees to supplement the ritual of question time, the House of Commons can perform to only a limited degree the function of accountability. As for protecting individual rights, Parliament has neither the time nor the machinery to perform that role adequately. In an age of complexity, of individual reliance on an intricate system of relationships with government, the role is increasingly important. But it can only be carried out effectively by the courts.

Conclusions

For all those reasons I think there will be growing support for a Bill of Rights enforceable in the courts of Britain. But it will have to overcome much resistance. As I discovered to my bewilderment long ago, people who in America welcome judicial protection of fundamental rights are instinctively sceptical here. They question the capacity of judges to perform that role.

No American could tell you with a straight face that the course of our constitutional law has been untroubled. But for all our differences we are confident that judges, working by the methods of legal reasoning, are best suited to the role of protecting individual rights. Judges have won that confidence by responding to the complexities of modern society – by developing new ways of applying old protections against the growing power and intrusiveness of the state.

In 1927 Justice Brandeis wrote that 'public discussion is a political duty', that 'the great menace to freedom is an inert people'. But he and Justice Holmes expressed their bold view of freedom of expression in dissent then. It was years before the experience of state power in the world made their view the prevailing one in the Supreme Court. In 1971 a justice who cherished traditional values, John Harlan, wrote for the court: 'The constitutional right of free expression is powerful medicine . . . It is designed to remove governmental restraints from the arena of public discussion . . . in the hope that use of such freedom will ultimately produce a more capable citizenry and more perfect polity. [In this sense it is] not a sign of weakness but of strength.'

If one believes in freedom of expression as Justice Harlan did, if one regards it as the sign of a self-confident society, then the advantage of writing it into a Bill of Rights is evident. The value of that freedom gradually asserts itself in the law. Judges, in the way of their work, come to take weightier account of freedom of speech and of the press.

The press is not always a noble beneficiary of its freedom. There are excesses in the United States as here: incursions on fair trial, to name a painful one. But I think the freedom has proved its value in the progressive and confident aspects of our imperfect country.

I leave the last word to a Frenchman, surely impartial. Alexis de Tocqueville visited America a few years before Dickens and, like him, found much to regret in the newspapers. In *Democracy in America* he quoted an outrageous press attack on President Jackson. Then he wrote: 'I admit that I do not feel toward freedom of the press the complete and instantaneous love which one affords to things by their nature supremely good. I love it more from considering the evils it prevents than on account of the good it does.'

No American could yet with a straight face that the course of our constitutional law has been untroubled, but for all our distrust we are content that judges, working by the methods of legal reasoning, are engaged in the role of protecting individual rights. Judges have won confidence by responding to the complexity of modern society, developing new ways of applying old protections against the growing power and intrusiveness of the state.

In 1927, Justice Brandeis wrote that public discussion is a political duty and the great menace to freedom is an inert people. But he and the

Spycatcher: Two Years of Legal Indignations

David Pannick

Spycatcher: The Book

'A secret agent who throws his secrecy to the winds from desire of vengeance, and flaunts his achievements before the public eye, becomes', as Joseph Conrad observed of Mr Verloc in *The Secret Agent*, 'the mark for desperate and bloodthirsty indignations'. By publishing his memoirs, *Spycatcher*, Peter Wright flaunted his dubious achievements in the security services and sought to gain his vengeance for the denial of the pension to which he thought himself entitled. The October 1988 judgment of the House of Lords – dismissing attempts to prevent further circulation of the book and its contents in this country – was the culmination of over two years' legal indignations on behalf of the British Government.

Spycatcher is, as Mr Justice Kirby observed in his judgment in the New South Wales Court of Appeal in September 1987, 'one rather cantankerous old man's perspective of things notorious, or description of technology long out-dated, people long since dead and controversies tirelessly worked over by numberless writers'. Yet, stimulated by an unprecedented series of legal actions across the world, *Spycatcher* has sold well over a million copies. As Alan Watkins commented in *The Observer*, the *Spycatcher* affair became as intricate and as baffling to outsiders as was the Schleswig-Holstein question to politicians in the nineteenth century. To appreciate the lessons it teaches, reference is required to the background and the history of this extraordinary saga.

Peter Wright joined MI5 in 1955. During the final three years of his employment from 1973 to 1976, he was a consultant to the Director-General, with particular responsibility for investigating Soviet infiltration into our

---

David Pannick is a Barrister and a Fellow of All Souls College, Oxford. In the Spycatcher *litigation, he acted for* The Sunday Times, The London Daily News *and* The South China Sunday Morning Post. *Most of this chapter was previously published in* The Times Literary Supplement *of 21 to 27 October 1988.*

Security Services. After his retirement, he moved to Australia. Prompted by a grievance over his pension entitlement and by an obsession that Sir Roger Hollis (Head of MI5 from 1955 to 1965) had been a Soviet agent, he wrote *Spycatcher*.

What the spy Kim Philby revealed to the British public about the activities of the Security Services in his autobiography *My Silent War* (1968) was, in parts, reassuring:

Sometimes, in the early weeks, I felt that perhaps I had not made the grade after all. It seemed that somewhere, lurking in deep shadow, there must be another service, really secret and really powerful, capable of backstairs machination on such a scale as to justify the perennial suspicions of, say, the French. But it soon became clear that such was not the case. It was the death of an illusion.

By contrast, Peter Wright did allege that there was indeed a *secret* Secret Service conducting operations which justified the suspicions not only of the French (whose Embassy in London was, he alleges, bugged during the abortive negotiations for Britain's entry into the Common Market in the early 1960s) but also of the Wilson Government of 1974 to 1976 (whose downfall was being plotted, he suggests, by at least one MI5 officer, that is himself).

Spycatcher: The Cases

In 1985 the British Government learnt of Heinemann's plan to publish *Spycatcher* in Australia and obtained an injunction from the Australian courts pending a trial of the legal issues between the parties. In June 1986, after *The Guardian* and *The Observer* published articles about that forthcoming trial, injunctions were obtained from the English courts against those newspapers.

By the summer of 1987, the Government's attempts to keep the book's contents secret had failed. The Cabinet Secretary, Sir Robert Armstrong, had an unhappy experience travelling to Australia to give evidence in the vain attempt to persuade Mr Justice Powell to impose a permanent injunction against publication in that country. The most interesting of Peter Wright's allegations were disclosed in *The Independent* in April 1987. In July 1987, *Spycatcher* was published in the USA. It was an immediate bestseller. The Prime Minister told Parliament that the Secretary of State for Trade and Industry had advised against an import ban 'because it is likely to be ineffective'.

Three English newspapers, *The Sunday Times, The Guardian* and *The Observer*, applied for the discharge of the English injunctions in the light of US publication. In *On the Run* (1987), the former CIA agent Philip Agee described how the CIA considered legal action in the USA to prevent publication of his 1975 book *Inside the Company*. William Colby, the CIA

Director, had tried to persuade the Justice Department to seek an injunction, 'but Justice said they couldn't get it because the book was already published in England.' Such a sensible approach, that one cannot realistically seek to rebottle secrets once they are out, did not commend itself to the British Government, or to some judges.

In ten extraordinary days of litigation in July 1987, the preliminary issues were considered by three English courts.[1] Sir Nicolas Browne-Wilkinson (the Vice-Chancellor) held that there was no longer any basis for an injunction against the newspapers. As he explained, 'in the contemporary world of electronics and jumbo jets, news anywhere is news everywhere'. He concluded that 'the law could . . . be justifiably accused of being an ass and brought into disrepute if it closed its eyes' to the reality that the book's contents were no longer secret, but easily obtainable by anyone who took the trouble to order a copy from the USA by post or telephone.

The Court of Appeal disagreed. Without being asked to do so by either the newspapers or the Attorney-General, it fashioned its own half-way house, allowing publication of 'a summary in very general terms of the allegations made by Mr Wright'. Then, the following week, in a strained atmosphere, the Law Lords concluded by a majority of three to two that there should be an injunction pending a full trial of the action against the newspapers. 'To attempt', as Lord Oliver observed in his dissenting speech, 'to create a sort of judicial cordon sanitaire against the infection from abroad of public comment and discussion is not only . . . certain to be ineffective, but involves taking the first steps upon a very perilous path.' Lord Bridge (former Chairman of the Security Commission) noted, in his dissenting speech, that 'freedom of speech is always the first casualty under a totalitarian regime'. By contrast, Lord Ackner – one of the judges in the majority – was concerned that the law should not cease to be a 'rock' and become a 'jellyfish'. Without being asked to do so by the Government, the judges in the majority extended the injunction to forbid the reporting of proceedings held in open court in Australia. The front-page comment in the *Daily Mirror*, 'You Fools', was more polite than the views expressed throughout the Temple on the wisdom of the majority decision.

In September 1987, the Attorney-General obtained an injunction from the Hong Kong Court of Appeal to prevent *The South China Sunday Morning Post* from publishing further extracts from the book. The Chinese language version, available in Peking, was beyond the Court's jurisdiction. *The Sun* – not previously known for the quality of its leaders on jurisprudential issues – observed that this was all 'Velly Silly'.

The full trial against *The Sunday Times*, *The Guardian* and *The Observer* to prevent those newspapers from publishing any information from *Spycatcher*, and to prevent *The Sunday Times* from serialising extracts from

---

1   [1987] 1 WLR 1248.

the book, began before Mr Justice Scott on 23 November 1987. In his opening speech, Robert Alexander Q.C., counsel for the Attorney-General, conceded, with admirable understatement, that 'as is well known, the Government has not been wholly successful in its objective of preventing any publication'.

Spycatcher: the Bestseller

By that time *Spycatcher* had been at the top of the bestseller lists in the USA and Canada for several weeks. The book had also been published in Australia and Ireland. Copies had been distributed throughout the world. A large number had been brought into the United Kingdom. Robert Alexander Q.C. informed Mr Justice Scott that 'on Friday evenings when there is always a queue on the [A40] there would always be one or two enterprising people who would jump out . . . They would hold up a copy of the book and say, "Want one?" '. Copies were not so easy to retain. 'My learned friend and my junior', Mr Alexander told Mr Justice Scott (as the official transcript records), 'have found that their copies have gone missing from the Court. [Laughter].'

Lengthy extracts had been printed by newspapers throughout the world: in London by *The Independent* and by *The Sunday Times*, by *The South China Morning Post* in Hong Kong, by *The Dominion* in New Zealand, by *The Daily Nation* in Kenya and by *Gulf News* in the United Arab Emirates. Danish Radio and Swedish Radio had broadcast extracts in English. Bookshops in Scotland were trying to avoid legal restrictions by giving away copies of the book with other works purchased, in one case a remaindered publication about Secretaries of State for Scotland, in another case with every copy bought of Prince Charles's *The Old Man of Lochnagar*. A record, 'Ballad of a Spycatcher', had been played several times on BBC Radio 1, repeating the major allegations. Peter Wright's literary agents in New York had sold the foreign language rights to publish *Spycatcher* in various translations, from Catalan to Icelandic.

The satirical television programme *Spitting Image* included a sketch in which it was suggested to the Prime Minister by one brave adviser that possibly the time had come to give up attempts to prevent people learning about the contents of *Spycatcher* since a musical by Andrew Lloyd-Webber based on the book had opened in the West End, and Torvill and Dean had created a new ice-dance routine around Wright's main allegations. A letter in *The Independent* asked whether the Attorney-General knew that the BBC was planning to broadcast the comedy film *Carry on Spying* and, if so, was he going to obtain an injunction?

Mr Justice Scott concluded that the publication by the newspapers of further information and extracts from the book could not cause any more damage to national security.[2] He found himself 'unable to escape the reflection that the

2   [1988] 2 WLR 805.

absolute protection of the Security Services that Sir Robert [Armstrong] was contending for could not be achieved this side of the Iron Curtain'.

The Court of Appeal dismissed the Government's appeal early in 1988.[3] As Lord Justice Bingham observed, 'the court will not seek to emulate the 15th-century pope who issued a papal bull against Halley's comet . . . Most of the great works of the French Enlightenment were, for good reason, published outside France. But the Bastille still fell.' Lord Justice Bingham wisely reminded us that 'Mr Wright's disservice to this country would . . . be compounded if revulsion from his conduct were to lead the law into paths not indicated by an objective application of settled and very important principles'.

On 2 June 1988, the High Court of Australia (that country's supreme judicial body) rejected the Government's claims for a financial remedy against Peter Wright and Heinemann. Contrary to the impression which many observers may have had at the time, and may still have after reading the account by Malcolm Turnbull, the lawyer who acted for Peter Wright and Heinemann ('the real damage to the British case had occurred during my cross-examination of Armstrong'),[4] the Australian case was not legally won or lost on the performance of Sir Robert Armstrong in the witness-box. The Australian courts refused to assist the British Government not because Sir Robert's evidence was disbelieved or found wanting, but because of a point of law, that the Australian legal system would not enforce what amounted to the public law of another State. Nor did any of the three Australian courts which heard the case accept the conspiracy theory of various events advanced on behalf of Peter Wright by Malcolm Turnbull.

Nevertheless, Turnbull's ritual humiliation of the pom sent down-under unsettled the British Government, provoked its public ridicule and un-doubtedly made it easier for the Australian judiciary to decide the case in favour of Peter Wright on a legal technicality.

Peter Wright was, in consequence, a millionaire. If the aim of the litigation had been to prevent him from profiting from his wrong, or to deter others, it had failed miserably. The Government's case had also been dismissed by the New Zealand courts.

The Government had recognised at an early stage in the saga that American and Canadian law – which provide constitutional protection for freedom of speech – offered no prospect of a remedy. By this time 1.5 million hardback copies of *Spycatcher* had been sold worldwide. Yet the Attorney-General was still asking the English courts to prevent English newspapers and bookshops informing their customers what people all over the world knew about *our* Security Services.

It was in this context that on 14 June 1988 the House of Lords began to hear the final appeal in the English proceedings. Alan Rusbridger, in his sketch in

---

3   *Ibid.*
4   Malcolm Turnbull, *The Spycatcher Trial*, Heinemann, 1988, at 196.

The Guardian, described how 'the Spycatcher Society held one of its periodic meetings in London yesterday . . . Those present were given an interesting talk on the history of the Wright affair by one of the world's leading scholars on the subject, Mr Robert Alexander, Q.C.'.

In their October 1988 judgment, the Law Lords put an end to the ridicule of the English law and confirmed what had been obvious since July 1987: that as a result of world-wide publication, all confidentiality in the contents of *Spycatcher* had been destroyed and no further harm could be done by publication in this country.[5]

The persistence of the Attorney-General in the *Spycatcher* litigation owed much to the widespread feeling that, by signing and fulfilling a publishing contract, Peter Wright was no better than a traitor. Obsession and spite are not more honourable motives than ideology. 'Those who have worked in intelligence,' said Noel Annan in his review of *Spycatcher* in *The New York Review of Books* in September 1987, 'will say Wright is a shit, and they will be right.' The Law Lords expressed similar sentiments. The most alarming aspect of the tale is that the Security Services should ever have employed a man whose political views were way to the right of the Conservative party and who saw Communist agents in (and not just under) every bed in Whitehall.

The ridiculous obsession of the British Government to prevent the British (and various other Commonwealth nations whose courts might prove sympathetic) from reading what the rest of the world already knew diverted the Government from an important task. The *Spycatcher* case established that should the Security Services again be incompetent enough to employ so unstable a person as Peter Wright, he could publish whatever he wished in the USA, Canada and Australia without legal impediment. In the House of Lords, Lord Keith sensibly suggested that 'consideration should be given to the possibility of some international agreement aimed at reducing the risks to collective security involved in the present state of affairs'. The Government should be devoting its legal expertise to devising with its allies a workable and principled system of prior vetting of the publications of Security Service insiders (comparable to that currently operated by the CIA) to ensure that the public is denied access only to a very limited range of material, publication of which would imperil national security.

There is no prospect that our allies would agree (or, in the case of the USA and Canada, could lawfully agree) to Treaty arrangements incorporated into their domestic law which prohibit the publication of *any* information about the British Secret Service written by an insider, the position adopted by the British Government throughout the *Spycatcher* case. Therefore, to secure such a Treaty − a vital need in the light of the *Spycatcher* experience − the Government must abandon its absolutist approach to such issues.

---

5   [1988] 3 WLR 776.

Free Speech: an American Comparison

English law is not at its best in defence of free speech. England is the libel capital of the world. Books, magazines and broadcasting are subject to obscenity laws more moralistic than anywhere else in Western Europe. Contempt of court law imposes restrictions on free speech which the legal systems of few other nations consider necessary or desirable to preserve the integrity of the legal process. The law of confidence has been expanded by the courts because of a belief that, in the words of Lord Justice Templeman in 1981, 'the times of Blackstone are not relevant to the times of Mr Murdoch'.[6]

The comparison with US law is instructive. American law, unlike English law, understands that freedom of expression means that editorial decisions on governmental matters are for editors, not for judges. A Treaty (if incorporated into US law) could prevent publication in the USA by the ex-MI5 officer.[7] It could not prevent publication in *The New York Times* or *The Washington Post*. The First Amendment to the US Constitution provides that 'Congress shall make no law . . . abridging the freedom of speech, or of the press'. As Mr Justice White explained in a 1974 judgment in the US Supreme Court, this 'erects a virtually insurmountable barrier between government and the print media so far as government tampering, in advance of publication, with news and editorial content is concerned'.[8]

In its two centuries of existence the US Supreme Court has never upheld a prior restraint on pure speech. So seriously does US law take free speech that in 1931 the Supreme Court suggested that an injunction *might* be possible in the context of national security in war-time in relation to 'the publication of the sailing dates of transports or the number and location of troops'.[9] In 1979, the US Government sought and obtained from a District Court an injunction to restrain publication by *The Progressive* magazine of an article informing readers how to manufacture an H-Bomb. Pending an appeal, another magazine published the same information. In consequence, the US moved to discharge the injunction it had obtained on the ground that the issue was now moot.[10] One can therefore understand the comment of Floyd Abrams, the leading First Amendment lawyer in the US, in his written evidence in the *Spycatcher* trial, that if the US courts were asked to decide whether a newspaper could publish the memoirs of a security service employee *after* they had already been published in other countries, 'these would not be difficult questions under American law; they would not be questions at all'.

---

6   *Schering Chemicals Ltd v Falkman Ltd* [1982] QB 1, 39.
7   See *Snepp v US* 444 US 507 (1980) (US Supreme Court).
8   *Miami Herald Publishing Co. v Tornillo* 418 US 241, 259 (1974).
9   *Near v Minnesota* 283 US 697, 716 (1931) (US Supreme Court).
10   *US v The Progressive Inc.* 486 F. Supp. 5 (1979) (US District Court); vacated by the US Court of Appeals on 1 October 1979.

US law gives such primacy to free speech for two reasons. The first is based on a principle of self-government and a recognition that freedom of information is central to the effective operation of a democracy. It is of limited value to citizens to give them the right to elect their representatives if those representatives can, by use of the legal process, deprive citizens of the information necessary to enable them to reach an informed judgement on the performance of their administration. As Madison observed in 1794, 'the censorial power is in the people over the Government, and not in the Government over the people'.[11]

The second reason for the primacy of free speech is a belief about effective decision-making. It is, implies the First Amendment, unacceptable for those in government to prevent the free circulation of ideas and information because this may prevent access to truth, or cover-up errors, inefficiency or plain corruption. Those who are troubled that this undiluted commitment to free speech may be incompatible with effective government need to recognise that the US has survived as the major world power notwithstanding – and perhaps at times (one has in mind the Watergate affair) because of – the First Amendment.

Of course, as Archibald Cox has written, 'some balance is inescapable. The ultimate question is always, Where has – and should – the balance be struck?'[12] Article 10 of the European Convention on Human Rights attempts to provide such a balance. It prohibits state interference with free speech unless there is a pressing social need for one of a limited number of defined purposes, such as national security. But no balancing test that respects the importance of free speech in a democracy could justify restraints on the publication in the United Kingdom of governmental information which has ceased to be secret because of its prior publication throughout the world. It is impossible to see how national security is involved at all, or sufficiently to override the need to allow the British to read what others know about their Government.

Implications for the Future

The implications of the judgments of the English courts in *Spycatcher* are profound for freedom of speech in the United Kingdom. Some of those implications are liberal. The courts have indicated that they are beginning to recognise that the principle of free speech as stated in Article 10 of the European Convention on Human Rights is part of English domestic law in the sense that, unless Parliament expressly requires to the contrary, the common law and statutory construction are to be assumed to further, rather than detract from, such fundamental rights.

---

11   Cited in Archibald Cox, *Freedom of Expression*, Harvard University Press, 1980, at 3.
12   *Ibid*, at 4.

Some of the implications are more conservative. The English judiciary adopts a narrow approach to the meaning of Article 10. But for US (and thereafter worldwide) publication, none of the Law Lords who heard the final appeal in 1988 would have allowed publication in the United Kingdom of information about the Security Services such as that contained in *Spycatcher*, despite the fact that what Wright describes is alleged to have occurred prior to (in many respects, well prior to) 1976, when he retired, and notwithstanding that he makes allegations of improper conduct by those in authority.

Those who are sighing with relief that *Spycatcher* and the law is a closed subject are mistaken. Important issues of free speech remain to be determined. The publication in *The Independent* in April 1987 of some of the *Spycatcher* allegations led to a prosecution for contempt of court of that newspaper and of two other newspapers, *The London Evening Standard* and *The London Daily News* (now deceased), which reported those disclosures.

In June 1987, the Vice-Chancellor agreed with the newspapers that it could not be a contempt of court for those three newspapers (which were not subject to an injunction) to publish what it knew *The Guardian* and *The Observer* had (in June 1986) been prohibited from publishing. In July 1987, the Court of Appeal allowed the Attorney-General's appeal.[13] Lord Justice Balcombe acknowledged that he was 'conscious that this conclusion is reached by a sophisticated argument which may not be readily apparent to the layman'. The question of whether those (and other) newspapers *had* committed a contempt was left for another day in court. In May 1989 three newspapers — *The Independent*, *The Sunday Times* and *The News on Sunday* — were found guilty of contempt by Mr Justice Morritt and each fined £50,000.[14] The issue of whether an injunction against one organ of the press effectively binds all other parts of the media is of obvious importance to the theory and practice of freedom of expression. The Law Lords may well be asked to resolve it.

The *Spycatcher* litigation began as high drama. By July 1987 it had turned into farce, with the Government caught with its trousers down in the Australian courts and seeking desperately to prevent what American publication had turned into a *fait accompli*. To many observers, the Court of Appeal and the majority of the Law Lords appeared in 1987, like fans of a James Bond film, to have suspended their critical faculties in order to accept far-fetched assertions about the requirements of national security in this espionage context. The affair was in serious danger of becoming a tragedy, with the reputation of the British legal system as the victim of what Chief Justice Davison in New Zealand called 'the most litigated book of all time'.

The *Spycatcher* litigation has, in fact, always been a monumental irrelevance to, and a dangerous distraction from, the genuine needs of national security. The hero of Graham Greene's *The Confidential Agent* realised that 'you could

---

13   [1987] 3 WLR 942.
14   *The Times*, 9 May 1989.

trust nobody but yourself, and sometimes you were uncertain whether after all you could trust yourself . . .'. Unless and until the British Government learns the lessons of *Spycatcher* – that it cannot now prevent publication in the USA, Canada and Australia, that it must devise a vetting system in co-operation with our allies to protect national security material, and that it is futile, absurd and a gross violation of freedom of expression to prevent the British public from reading any material written by an insider, especially when it is widely available elsewhere in the world – the British Government will remain undeserving of trust in this context.

The Spycatcher Saga: Public Secrecy from Private Rights*

Rodney Austin

The glare of sensational media publicity surrounding the *Spycatcher* saga[1] has tended to obscure a major legal development in the area of official secrecy, namely the use by the Government of private law rights and remedies to restrict publication of official information. Although *Spycatcher* has commanded most of the media's interest and public attention, the Government has resorted to private law to restrain publication of another book of memoirs by a retired intelligence agent,[2] of a book of memoirs by a female under-cover wartime resistance agent,[3] of a television programme concerning the development of the 'Zircon' spy satellite,[4] and of a serious and responsible BBC radio programme concerning the intelligence and security services.[5]

The purpose of this paper is to examine the recent attempts by government to enforce its private law rights under the laws of contract, confidentiality, fiduciary duty and copyright, by means of private law remedies such as

Rodney Austin LL.B. Hons. (NZ) Barrister and Solicitor in the High Court New Zealand, Senior Lecturer, Law Faculty, University College London

* This essay is a much revised version of a 1988 staff seminar presentation at UCL Law Faculty, and of a later paper presented at the Law and Politics Colloquium, Bristol University, May 1988. I am grateful for the many constructive comments and helpful advice of my colleagues but they do not bear any responsibility for any deficiencies in this paper, which remains mine alone.

1   The interlocutory proceedings for temporary injunctions are reported as *AG v Guardian Newspapers* [1987] 2 All ER 316 (Ch D, CA & HL). The proceedings for permanent injunctions are reported as *AG v Guardian Newspapers (No. 2)* [1988] 2 All ER 545 (Ch D, CA & HL). The contempt proceedings in which the original interlocutory injunctions were held to apply to other newspapers not party to the original proceedings are reported as *AG v Newspaper Publishing plc* [1987] 3 All ER 276 (Ch D & CA). The Australian proceedings are reported as *AG (UK) v Heinemann Publishers Australia Pty Ltd* [1987] 8 NSWLE 341 (NSWSC); (1987) 75 ALR 353 (NSWCA); (1988) 78 ALR 449 (Aust. HC). The New Zealand proceedings are *AG v Wellington Newspapers Ltd* (28 April 1988, as yet unreported). The Hong Kong proceedings are unreported, but see [1988] 2 All ER 545, 557.

2   'Inside Intelligence', by Cavendish.

3   'One Girl's War' by Joan Miller.

4   'The Secret Society', a BBC series; the particular programme was by the journalist Duncan Campbell.

5   A BBC Radio 4 series entitled 'My Country, Right or Wrong'.

injunctions and orders to account for profits. By analysis and discussion of the decisions in these cases, this paper will seek the reasons for this sudden upsurge in the Government's use of private law and examine the legitimacy of this relatively new phenomenon. It will then suggest that public authorities ought to be precluded from relying on private law rights and remedies to enforce what are in reality essentially public law obligations, or that where private law is used to enforce such public law concerns, those private law concepts and remedies require substantial modifications so as to ensure that their use is appropriate in the public law context.

Use of Private Law Concepts and Remedies

Although the public may be familiar with the popular history of the *Spycatcher* saga, it is instructive to examine the legal background to these and other attempts by government to restrain publication through private law. Peter Wright, a former MI5 agent, now resident in Australia, wrote a book of his memoirs of his time in MI5, which was to be published by Heinemann, the publishing company, in the UK and Australia, and by Viking Penguin in the USA. The UK Government immediately sought and obtained various interlocutory injunctions restraining the publication of the book, of any extracts therefrom or any report of the contents thereof, against the original publishers, against a number of newspapers and eventually, through judicial innovation, against almost the world at large.[6] These interim injunctions were granted by courts in the UK,[7] in the colony of Hong Kong,[8] in the State of New South Wales in Australia[9] and in New Zealand.[10] Despite this initial success, however, the Government's efforts were doomed to ultimate failure when it sought to have the injunctions made permanent.[11] During these long-drawn-out legal battles, publication of the book went ahead in the UK, through private import which the Government declined to prevent,[12] through public sale by a limited number of bookshops[13] and through inclusion in the stock of public libraries.[14]

---

6   Contempt proceedings brought by the AG against other newspapers not party to the original temporary injunctions were upheld by the Court of Appeal against *The Independent* and *The Sunday Times*, on the grounds that publication by them would frustrate the purpose of and render worthless the original injunctions. See Note 1 above for references.
7   See Note 1 above for reference.
8   *Ibid.*
9   *Ibid.*
10   *Ibid.*
11   *Ibid.*
12   There is some doubt as to whether the powers of the Government under existing legislation would permit the prohibition of importation of the book; see [1988] 3 All ER 545, at 595, per Donaldson MR. See also [1988] 3 All ER 545 at 557 to 558, per Scott J.
13   See [1988] 3 All ER 545 at 557, per Scott J. The AG wrote to UK bookshops warning them not to sell the book, but some continued to do so.
14   See *AG v Observer Ltd* [1988] 1 All ER 385.

The basis of the Government's claim for injunctions to restrain publication was that as a consequence of his undertaking to keep secret everything he learnt in the course of his employ with MI5, Mr Wright owed a lifelong duty of absolute confidentiality.[15] This duty was either contractual, equitable or fiduciary in origin, its breach could be restrained by injunction and any profits arising from publication could be recovered by the Government. Further, third parties owed the Government a duty to respect the obligation of confidence owed by Wright to the Government, a duty which was enforceable by injunction to restrain publication and an order to account for profits. Furthermore, although not party to the proceedings for injunctions to restrain publication, any other person who, knowing of the injunctions, published the information specified in the injunctions, could be punished for contempt and restrained by injunction from any further publication.[16]

The Crown's right to confidentiality arose from the employment relationship with Mr Wright. Initially the Crown sought to rely on contract but this was obviously a weak basis, since Wright was employed at pleasure under the royal prerogative of defence of the realm, hardly a very likely source of contract.[17]

But the absence of a contract does not preclude the existence of enforceable obligations arising from the employment relationship, in particular equitable and fiduciary obligations, nor of a special right vested in the Crown to restrain the publication of material the disclosure of which would be contrary to the public interest because such disclosure would prejudice national security. This latter right arises from the nature of the information itself rather than from the employment or other relationship.[18] The Government did not seek to rely on this latter right, because the contents of the book did not contain material the disclosure of which could directly prejudice national security.[19] Much of the information was out-of-date, either in terms of the intelligence services' structure, organisation, methodology and personnel, or in terms of the technology utilised for intelligence-gathering and counter-intelligence surveillance and monitoring. Much of the information was no longer secret, having been widely publicised in earlier books[20] – the Government took no action whatsoever to restrain publication of these for reasons which included the fact that it had surreptitiously obtained a pre-publication copy from the publishers and had been legally advised that there were no grounds upon which it could seek to restrain publication.[21] (Such advice is and was at the time so patently wrong, in the light of the *Crossman Diaries*[22] case, that one

---

15 See [1988] 3 All ER 545, 566 to 568, per Scott J.
16 See Notes 1 and 6 above.
17 See [1988] 3 All ER 545, 573, per Scott J.
18 An obvious and related parallel is of course found in the law's recognition and enforcement of 'content' claims for public interest immunity; see *Conway v Rimmer* [1968] AC 910.
19 See [1988] 3 All ER 545, 567 to 568, per Scott J.
20 See [1988] 3 All ER 545, 558 to 564, per Scott J.
21 See [1988] 3 All ER 545, 560 to 561, per Scott J.
22 *AG v Jonathan Cape Ltd* [1975] 3 All ER 484.

suspects there may have been other reasons for not acting to restrain the earlier publications.)

Whatever the reason, the Government's failure to act against the earlier publications had two consequences, first that any claim that disclosure of the contents of Mr Wright's book would endanger national security was rendered untenable, second that one of the essential ingredients of a successful claim for protection of confidence, viz. that the information has the necessary character of confidentiality, was severely prejudiced or diminished.[23]

Nevertheless, with the contract and national security bases for the action effectively eliminated the Government had to fall back on the equitable or fiduciary obligations of confidentiality arising from the employment relationship.[24] The difficulties for the Government in pursuing the equitable confidentiality basis for the action were twofold. First, that much of the information was already in the public domain, and therefore lacked the necessary character of confidence, and second, that the application of the doctrine of confidence to governmental information in the *Crossman Diaries*[25] case and the subsequent *Fairfax*[26] case in Australia had introduced an additional requirement, namely that the Government had to establish that there was a public interest in keeping the information secret, and that such public interest outweighed any countervailing public interest in having the information made public.[27] In the absence of any contents/national security basis for secrecy, the Government was thus forced to fall back on the general propositions that it was in the public interest for the efficient and effective working of the security and intelligence services that all and any information about them be kept secret, because disclosure might weaken the morale of those working in the services, (a parallel can be found in the largely discredited 'class claims' for public interest immunity), and that if Mr Wright's memoirs could be published, other former agents might also be tempted to rush into print. (The *pour encourager les autres* justification).[28]

Looked at in the cold light of legal analysis, the Government's case against the publication of much of the information in Mr Wright's book looked fairly

---

23   See [1988] 3 All ER 545, 564, 587 to 589 and 592 to 593, per Scott J.
24   (The copyright basis was never a realistic ground, since the book did not actually reproduce government documents, and the Government formally abandoned that ground during the proceedings.) Furthermore, copyright law permits selective quotations under the fair dealing exception, so that newspapers could not have been prohibited from revealing some of the information in the book. But Scott J and a number of the other judges considered that copyright could have provided the basis for an injunction; see [1988] 3 All ER 545, 567 and 593, per Scott J; 621, per Dillon LJ; 647, per Lord Brightman; 654, per Lord Griffiths; 645, per Lord Keith; But at 609, Donaldson MR rejects copyright as the basis.
25   Note 22 above supra.
26   *Commonwealth of Australia v John Fairfax and Sons Ltd* (1980) 32 ALR 485, (Aust. HC).
27   [1975] 3 All ER 484, 495 to 496, per Lord Widgery CJ. (1980) 32 ALR 485, 492 to 493, per Mason J.
28   [1988] 3 All ER 545, 568, per Scott J; 616, per Dillon LJ; 631 to 632, per Bingham LJ; 642, per Lord Keith; 653 to 654, per Lord Griffiths.

thin, and Scott J, the Court of Appeal and the House of Lords[29] took a similar view. In addition, since the injunction is an equitable and hence discretionary remedy, the maxim that 'Equity will not act in vain' applied so that the courts would exercise their discretion and decline to grant an injunction to bolt the stable door long after the horse had bolted, that is, now that the information was already in the public domain.[30]

A significant and disturbing feature of the first instance, Court of Appeal and House of Lords decisions is that although the courts declined to grant injunctions against the newspapers concerned, it was made abundantly clear that had the Government been seeking injunctions against Mr Wright, or his publishers Heinemann, the courts would have taken a very different view.[31] The judges all regarded Mr Wright as bound by his continuing direct obligation of confidence, and Heinemann as being bound to respect that obligation. In principle, therefore, the Government won its case in so far as it was seeking to establish the general proposition that members of the security and intelligence services owed the Crown a lifelong and near-absolute duty of confidence in respect of information acquired in the course of their service. Only in rare and extreme circumstances would that duty be overridden by any public interest in disclosure.[32] Thus future books on the security and intelligence services and on other aspects of Government involving sensitive information, written by former members of the services or by other civil servants, could be restrained from publication by injunction for breach of confidence.

Having briefly chronicled the legal saga, I now turn to the issues which it is the purpose of this essay to explore, namely why did the Government resort to the private law of confidence and the private law remedy of injunction, and what are the implications of its so doing?

First, why did the Government seek to utilise the private law of confidence? (After its initial foray into the field in the *Crossman Diaries* case in 1976, nearly a decade elapsed before Government again resorted to confidence in the *Spycatcher* case.) The reasons are numerous. Prosecution or the threat thereof for breach of the Official Secrets Act 1911, section 2, was, as in the *Crossman Diaries* case, unworkable. Just as the dead cannot be prosecuted, so too Mr Wright was equally immune, being outside the jurisdiction. Although section 2 has extra-territorial application to the acts of disclosure,[33] the

---

29   *Ibid.*
30   [1988] 3 All ER 545, 592 to 593, per Scott J; 610, per Donaldson MR; 616, per Dillon LJ; 642 to 643, per Lord Keith; 647 to 648, per Lord Brightman; 666, per Lord Goff.
31   [1988] 3 All ER 545, 586 and 593, per Scott J; 597 to 598, per Donaldson MR; 613, per Dillon LJ; 633, per Bingham LJ; 642, per Lord Keith; 647, per Lord Brightman; 651, per Lord Griffiths; 661 to 667, per Lord Goff.
32   [1988] 3 All ER 545, 585 to 586 per Scott J; 598, per Donaldson MR; 650 per Lord Griffiths; 660, per Lord Goff.
33   Official Secrets Act 1911, section 10; the Act applies to acts committed anywhere by Her Majesty's subjects.

courts do not have jurisdiction to try and convict persons not within the jurisdiction. Nor could Mr Wright be returned forcibly to the UK since breach of section 2 is not an extraditable offence nor is it subject to the Fugitive Offenders Act 1967.[34]

Further, the Government had suffered a major defeat in its previous attempt to prosecute a civil servant for disclosure of official information where the disclosure did not directly prejudice national security and where there was arguably a public interest in disclosure, the *Ponting* trial.[35] No doubt Mr Wright, if prosecuted, would, like Clive Ponting, appeal to the public interest in disclosure of the many allegations of wrongdoing, illegality, incompetence and mismanagement by and of the security services, contained in his book. The earlier *ABC* trial,[36] relating to disclosures about Signals Intelligence ('Sigint') and General Communications Headquarters (GCHQ) had also inflicted a symbolic defeat on the Government, because most of the information disclosed by the journalists was already in the public domain. The prosecution had received a public rebuke from the bench for attempting to prosecute the defendants under section 1 of the Official Secrets Act 1911, the espionage provisions. Since much of the material in *Spycatcher* was already in the public domain, it might prove equally disastrous for the Government to prosecute.

Technically, a willing recipient of offical information can also be prosecuted under section 2,[37] so the newspapers, their editors and the journalists could have been prosecuted or threatened therewith. But it could well prove to be politically unpopular, even fatal, for a government to start prosecuting respectable newspaper publishers and their editors and journalists. So prosecution was neither possible in Mr Wright's case nor a politically viable option in the newspapers' case.

Another possible option open to the Government might have been to use the D-Notice[38] machinery under which the Services, Press and Broadcasting Committee would issue a notice to the media indicating that the material in Mr Wright's book should not be published. The difficulty here is that the committee will issue a D-Notice only where it is satisfied that publication of the material itself will prejudice the defence or security of the realm, a test which the material in *Spycatcher* would, by the Government's admission, not satisfy. The D-Notice system is designed to prevent specific harm, rather than to uphold general governmental secrecy.

---

34   Fugitive Offenders Act 1967, section 3 and Schedule 1; Extradition Act 1870, First Schedule.
35   See Clive Ponting, *The Right to Know*, Sphere Books, 1985.
36   See Michael, *The Politics of Secrecy,* Pelican Books, 1982 at 50 to 59.
37   Official Secrets Act 1911, section 2(2).
38   See Michael, *op. cit.* at 86 to 89, for a brief description of the D-Notice system. See Williams, *Not in the Public Interest*, Hutchinson, 1965, at 80 to 88 for a more detailed discussion.

A further mechanism the Government might normally rely on to muzzle civil servants is the use of sanctions under the Civil Service Discipline Code of the Establishment Officers Guide (formerly known as 'Estacode'), the internal disciplinary rules by which civil servants are governed.[39] Two difficulties arise here; first, it is not clear whether the guide applies to security service employees, since they fall outside the establishment Home Civil Service (Wright, for example, lost his Civil Service pension when he transferred from the Admiralty to MI5).[40] Second, disciplinary action or the threat thereof may be effective against civil servants still in employment in the Service, but it is difficult to discipline retired members, especially at a distance of 12,000 miles. The sanction of withdrawal of pension might normally be available, but in Wright's case he had, as mentioned, lost his pension rights upon transfer to MI5, and had apparently been badly treated in that respect, contrary to earlier assurances by MI5, upon his retirement.[41] Furthermore, the sanction of pension withdrawal might have precisely the reverse effect to that intended, by providing added incentive to publish in order to recoup some money to compensate for the loss! One suspects that Mr Wright himself may well have been provoked to act as he did because of the alleged manner in which his pension rights were treated.

So the various possible public law and administrative devices to restrain or discourage publication did not look particularly encouraging to the Government. What advantages would a private law action for injunction to restrain breach of confidence offer?

First, private law is capable of extra-territorial enforcement. Unlike criminal law, private law obligations can be enforced in foreign courts if the defendant is resident abroad or if the breach occurs abroad, provided the law in the foreign jurisdiction recognises the same or substantially similar rights and obligations. Since Australia is a common law and equity jurisdiction, its courts recognise and apply the same law of confidence as applies in the UK. So private law offered the UK Government the opportunity to restrain Mr Wright and his publishers from publishing in Australia.

Secondly, the burden of proof in a civil action is of a lower standard than in criminal prosecutions, being the balance of probabilities rather than proof beyond all reasonable doubt. If the Government was required to establish that the public interest would be damaged by publication, the balance of probabilities test would be easier to satisfy than the criminal burden of proof.

Third, the trial of a civil action is by judge alone, with no jury. This would no doubt be particularly appealing to the Government after the *Ponting*[42] verdict, which, in legal terms, was clearly perverse. Judges are probably less

---

39 The Government explicitly refers to the use of the Disciplinary Code in the White Paper on Reform of section 2 of the Official Secrets Act 1911, Cmnd 408/1988, at 15, paragraphs 71 to 73.

40 Peter Wright, *Spycatcher*, Viking Penguin, 1987, at 25 to 26.

41 Wright, *op. cit.,* at 367.

42 Ponting, *op. cit.*

likely than jurors to ignore or reject the law merely because they believe it is a bad law, and judges' errors, being appealable, lack the finality and sanctity of jury verdicts.

Fourth, the private law of confidence applies to third parties, however remote in the chain of recipients of information.[43] Section 2 of the Official Secrets Act 1911 does apply to a willing recipient of official information,[44] but it is doubtful whether section 2 continues to apply to recipients beyond the first, direct recipient in the chain of disclosure.[45] The law of confidence continues to apply to restrain publication by any person, however far down the chain, if the information has originally been disclosed in breach of confidence.

Fifthly, the law of confidence offers the major benefit of prior restraint by injunction, whereas prosecution under section 2 of the Official Secrets Act 1911 is a post-disclosure sanction. Technically, of course, the Attorney-General can seek an injunction to restrain the commission of a criminal offence,[46] but in the case of those who are not servants or agents of the Crown, that is, the publishers and the newspapers, the only offence is receipt of information, not its publication.[47] It is therefore highly doubtful whether the A-G would succeed in an action for an injunction to restrain publication by the newspapers, since their publication of the contents of Mr Wright's book would not be an offence under section 2.

These, then, may have been the reasons for the course of action taken by the UK Government. In the event, its calculations went badly astray. In Australia, following the *Crossman Diaries*[48] and *Fairfax*[49] decisions, the courts held[50] that confidence claims by government require the application of a different test from that applied where a private employer seeks to enforce confidence. The burden of proof lies on the Government to prove a public interest in non-disclosure, and that test must first be satisfied before the Government's case can go any further. Even if that test is satisfied, the public interest in non-disclosure must then be weighed against any claim by the

---

43 Indeed, it is frequently the case that the plaintiff is seeking to restrain widespread publication by third parties, usually the media, rather than by the original confidant, for example, *Lion Laboratories v Mirror Group Newspapers* [1984] 2 All ER 408; *British Steel v Granada Television* [1981] 1 All ER 417; *AG v Jonathan Cape* [1975] 3 All ER 484; *Argyll v Argyll* [1965] 1 All ER 611.

44 Official Secrets Act 1911, section 2(2).

45 Official Secrets Act 1911, section 2(2), specifies that the information must have been communicated in contravention of the Act. Section 2(1) of the Act applies to communications by Crown servants or contractors. Thus a further communication of information by the original recipient, not being a Crown servant or contractor, cannot create liability for the further recipient, under section 2(2).

46 See, for example, *Gouriet v Union of Post Office Workers* [1978] AC 435.

47 Section 2(1), Official Secrets Act 1911, specifies that communication must be by a Crown servant or agent.

48 Above, Note 22.

49 Above, Note 26.

50 See Note 1 for references to the Australian decisions.

defendant of a public interest in disclosure.[51] There was, in Australia, a public interest in disclosure because MI5 intelligence was supplied to and used by the Australian Security and Intelligence Service (SIS) and in particular, because the SIS was created under the supervision of Sir Roger Hollis, the MI5 Director identified by Mr Wright in his book as a Soviet agent, the infamous 'mole' in MI5. That public interest clearly outweighed any public interest in keeping the contents of the book secret. The Australian Courts further held,[52] in a perceptive analysis of the UK Government's case, that the private law of confidence could not be used to enforce the criminal law of another state. To do so would be contrary to the Australian public interest.

In the UK, the courts at first instance and on appeal,[53] adopted the Australian courts' reasoning in respect of publication by newspapers in the UK of some of the allegations contained in *Spycatcher*, because the public interest in disclosure of that specific information through a free press in a democratic society outweighed the relatively low public interest in keeping the information secret. But, the publication of serialised extracts by one of the newspapers was in breach of the obligation of confidence, and although the courts would not enjoin further publication of such extracts (because of the subsequent worldwide publication of the book) they would order that newspaper to account to the Attorney-General for the profits it had made from that earlier publication. Furthermore, the breach of confidence by Mr Wright and his publishers precluded their seeking the assistance of the courts to enforce their copyright. Anyone is now free to publish *Spycatcher*.[54]

It is to be noted that these rather liberal rulings on future publication did not apply to Mr Wright and his publishers. Even now, if Mr Wright or his publishers sought to publish *Spycatcher* in the UK it is clear from the judgments[55] that the Government would succeed in an action for an injunction to restrain publication, and an order to account for profits including, possibly, the profits from sales abroad. The public interest defence, available to the newspapers who publish information from the book, would not, apparently, be available to Mr Wright or his publishers. With respect, this seems an illogical position to arrive at, since the public interest in disclosure depends upon the nature and content of the information, not the identity of the discloser. It is also contrary to the earlier *Lion Intoximeter*[56] decision, where the discloser, an employee of the plaintiff, was able to claim the public

---

51 Formerly known as the iniquity test, now expanded by, for example, the *Lion Intoximeter* decision; see *Lion Laboratories v Evans* [1984] 2 All ER 417.
52 *AG (UK) v Heinemann Publishers Australia Ltd* (1987) 75 ALR 353, 404 per Kirby P, and 448, per McHugh JA.
53 See Note 1 above for references.
54 [1988] 3 All ER 545, 645, per Lord Keith; 648, per Lord Brightman; 654, per Lord Griffiths; 668, per Lord Jauncey.
55 See Note 31 above.
56 Above, Note 51.

interest defence, as was the newspaper which sought to publish the material he had disclosed.

The Public Law/Private Law Divide

Just over a century ago, Dicey,[57] whose influence on constitutional thought still pervades the halls of learning and the courts of law, argued that in Britain there is no separation of public law and private law, that all persons, whether private citizens or public officials, were equally subject to the ordinary law adjudicated upon by the ordinary courts. The English lawyer's deeply rooted hostility to and suspicion of separate governmental courts, based on the experience of the Star Chamber, coloured Dicey's perception of the French droit administratif, tribunaux administratifs and Conseil d'Etat. Such institutions in his view put public officials in a privileged position, above the law. Dicey preferred the view of the 17th century common law, echoed by Lord Denning in this century: 'Be you ever so high, the law is above you.'[58]

But as Professor Zellick has pointed out,[59] the view that the Government is no different from the private citizen can have unfortunate consequences, as shown by the *Malone*[60] telephone-tapping case. If government is able to exercise the same legal rights as any private citizen, the law of contract can be utilised, as Daintith has shown,[61] in ways which might not be thought appropriate for public authorities. Recent judicial appreciation of this phenomenon has resulted in the beginnings of a separate public law of contract, evidenced in the *Wheeler*[62] and *Shell Oil*[63] decisions.

In Administrative law, the judicial perception of a need to distinguish between public law and private law has been apparent and given effect for nearly two decades. In the field of liability for negligence, the House of Lords first conceived the special character of public law in the *Dorset Yacht*[64] case, gave full effect to the distinction in *Anns v London Borough of Merton*,[65] and created a further limitation on the liability of public authorities in *Curran v Northern Ireland Housing Executive*.[66] In the area of estoppel, apart from a valiant effort by Lord Denning to protect the victim of broken promises,[67]

---

57   Dicey, *Introduction to the Study of the Law of the Constitution* (1885). References are to the 10th edn, 1960, by ECS Wade, at 202 to 203.
58   *Gouriet v Union of Post Office Workers* [1977] 1 All ER 696 (CA), 718, per Lord Denning MR, quoting Thomas Fuller.
59   Zellick, 'Government Beyond Law' [1985] PL 283.
60   *Malone v Metropolitan Police Commissioner* [1979] Ch 344.
61   Daintith, 'Regulation by Contract: The New Prerogative' (1979) 32 CLP 41.
62   *Wheeler v Leicester City Council* [1985] AC 1054.
63   *R v Lewisham LBC, Ex p. Shell UK* [1988] 1 All ER 938.
64   *Dorset Yacht v Home Office* [1970] AC 1004.
65   [1978] AC 728.
66   [1987] 2 All ER 13 (HL).
67   *Robertson v Minister of Pensions* [1949] 1 KB 227; *Lever Finance v Westminster City LBC* [1971] 1 QB 222.

the courts have consistently recognised a special public law privilege against being bound by statements or undertakings given by public officials.[68]

The courts have long recognised the special position of public authorities in relation to discovery of documents in litigation, giving effect to that recognition by way of the doctrine of public interest immunity,[69] recently strengthened in favour of public authorities.[70]

More recently, the House of Lords explicitly recognised the peculiarly public law character of challenges to the exercise of public law powers and reserved exclusive jurisdiction over such disputes to the Divisional Court by way of application for judicial review.[71]

In each of these instances of judicial recognition of the special position of public authorities, the courts have granted public authorities a special privilege or immunity from the *ordinary* law as it normally applies to a private citizen. In every case, the public authority is in a favoured position, to the detriment of the private individual. It is of course true that, to some extent, Administrative law also imposes some special public law duties and obligations upon public authorities which are not imposed upon private individuals, precisely because of the public character of the functions of those public authorities. In some cases however those obligations and duties have been imposed upon private bodies and individuals exercising quasi-public power over others, for example, employers, trade unions, trade and professional associations, self-regulating organisations.

The thesis of this essay is that since public authorities, contrary to the traditional Diceyan view, have been given specially favourable immunities and privileges, because of the public character of their duties and functions, then logically and in fairness, they should be denied the use of purely private law rights and remedies to enforce public law obligations or to vindicate public law claims.

As applied to the law of confidence, this would preclude the use of the private law to enforce obligations of non-disclosure by employees in order to protect the public interest. Since public bodies do possibly have some private life there may of course be cases where the Government or other public authority would be seeking to enforce a purely private duty of confidence, as, for example, where a Government employee seeks to sell commercial information for private gain, for example, a MAFF scientific adviser who passes on valuable information on a new product, such as a plant variety, which the Government intends to market and sell for financial gain. This would be, in essence, a private law matter to which the private law should

---

68   *Western Fish Products v Penwith DC* [1981] 2 All ER 204, *Rootkin v Kent CC* [1981] 1 WLR 1186.

69   *Duncan v Cammell Laird* [1942] AC 624, modified by *Conway v Rimmer* [1968] AC 910 and *Burmah Oil v Bank of England* [1980] AC 1090.

70   *Air Canada v Secretary of State for Trade* [1983] 2 AC 394.

71   *O'Reilly v Mackman* [1983] 2 AC 237.

continue to apply. But when government seeks to vindicate secrecy in the name of the public interest, then it is clearly inappropriate that government be able to resort to private law in the shape of actions for breach of confidence. Although the courts have, as shown by the *Spycatcher* case, adapted the private law of confidence to some extent to suit the special character of a claim for secrecy in the public interest, this does not, it is submitted, meet all the deficiencies in the private law system when utilised in the public law context.

It would be more appropriate to create a separate public law power to restrain the disclosure of confidential information, with some formal machinery to operate the appropriate tests. The D-Notice system springs to mind as a model, though it would have to be expanded to apply to a wider range of information than that whose disclosure would prejudice national security or defence of the realm. Secondly, it would need to be placed on a statutory basis rather than its present voluntary, non-enforceable, non-statutory basis so as to avoid unenforceable decisions being ignored and ineffective in practice. Alternatively, reform of section 2 of the Official Secrets Act 1911 could include special powers for the Attorney-General to seek an injunction to restrain a prospective branch of the new provisions. He has such a power at common law to prevent the commission of crimes, but it is an unreviewable prerogative power.[72] Putting this power on a statutory basis would clarify its scope, and the Attorney-General could be required to meet the criminal burden of proof, to establish the public interest in non-disclosure and the absence of any counter-weight public interest in disclosure. He would also have to establish that the seriousness of the damage likely to be caused by disclosure justified prior restraint rather than *ex post facto* punitive sanctions. It might also be advisable to require a jury in such cases, in order to overcome the tendency of some judges to be 'more executive minded than the Executive',[73] when dealing with official secrecy.[74]

A further alternative to either of the above proposals would be the establishment of formal machinery for determining whether material sought to be disclosed by present or former civil servants (including members of the security and intelligence services) should or should not be disclosed.[75] Such a body could authorise publication in whole or in part, it could order deletion of material it thought improper to disclose, or it could refuse to permit any disclosure at all, on the grounds that all the material was of such a nature that its disclosure would be likely to cause harm to one or more of the governmental interests identified as justifying restrictions on disclosure. Disclosure contrary to the findings of such a body would then *prima facie* be a breach of the public duty of confidence or in some limited classes of case, a criminal

---

72   *Gouriet v Union of Post Office Workers* [1978] AC 435 (HL).
73   *Liversidge v Anderson* [1942] AC 206, 244, per Lord Atkin.
74   For example, *R v Home Secretary, Ex p. Hosenball* [1977] 3 All ER 452, the *Ponting* trial summing-up (see Ponting, *op. cit.*), *Chandler v DPP* [1964] AC 763.
75   Such machinery exists in the USA and France.

offence under the reformed Official Secrets Act.[76] The findings and conclusions of such a body would put third parties on notice that the material was subject to restrictions, so that publishers would know whether by publishing they ran the risk of exposing themselves to orders restraining publication or more seriously, prosecutions for criminal offences.

It might be suggested that the ultimate failure of all the actions taken by the Government to restrain publication of *Spycatcher*, the *Secret Society* television programme, the *My Country Right or Wrong* radio programme and the two other books by former members of the security and intelligence services indicates that the private law of confidence, as adapted by the courts to suit its use in the public law context, is proving to be less restrictive than feared and a wholly appropriate medium for the courts to weigh the competing public interests in disclosure and non-disclosure. This would, however, be a misleading impression: first, because it is abundantly clear from their Lordships' judgments in the *Spycatcher* case[77] that they wholly supported the Government in principle, even if they felt unable to support the Government's attempt in that case to plug an empty sink. It is therefore highly likely that the Government will be able to use the law of confidence in future to restrain publication of books by other civil servants. Second, although the courts claim that they impartially weigh the public interest in disclosure, and that the Government has the burden of proof to establish the need for restraining publication,[78] the courts' record in this general field of official information is at best variable and at worst highly deferential to government claims of questionable merit.[79]

Third, the lowered burden of proof in civil cases provides the Government with a relatively easy threshold to cross, especially in the absence of a jury, in order to restrict a fundamental freedom in a democracy.

Fourth, the application of a concept designed to protect private and commercial interests in the context of a modern democratic government acting as the promoter, guardian and instrument of the public interest or interests, seems constitutionally incongruous and inapt.

This lack of confidence in or mistrust of the Government's ability to have recourse to the private law might be lessened if the constitutional and public law mechanisms for control of the executive were more effective. The doctrine of ministerial responsibility is at best a 'frail barque'[80] in which to set sail, and in the area of national security, in particular the operation of the security and intelligence services, it has sunk almost without trace. The Prime Minister,

---

76   See Official Secrets Act 1989, section 7.
77   See Note 31 above.
78   See *AG v Jonathan Cape* [1975] 3 All ER 484, 495 to 596, per Lord Widgery, approved in *AG v Guardian (No. 2)* [1988] 3 All ER 545, 575 to 578, per Scott J.
79   For example, *Air Canada v Secretary of State for Trade*, above.
80   Harlow and Rawlings, *Law and Administration*, Weidenfeld & Nicolson, 1984, at 42.

nominally responsible for those services,[81] and the Home and Foreign Secretaries under whose departments the services function in practice, are extremely reticent about the operations, personnel and funding thereof. Questions in the House are either refused outright or at best, answered in a very general and largely uninformative manner. Neither the Home nor Foreign Affairs Select Committees exercise any form of scrutiny, supervision or control over the services. There is no standing parliamentary body to whom the services are accountable or responsible, and the Government in 1988 expressly rejected calls to set up any form of supervisory or scrutiny body, when putting the security services on a statutory footing.[82]

Similarly, legal controls over issues of national security and the security services are equally weak. Faced with a claim of national security, the courts reduce the scope and penetration of judicial review to a formal minimum.[83] The present criminal law on disclosure of information identifies 'Interest of the State' with the interests of or as defined by, the government of the day,[84] thus leaving no real room for a defence based on notions of public, national or wider state interests, separate and distinct from the executive government's interests. Equally, judicial scrutiny of the issuance of warrants for interception of communications and search warrants for execution by the security services has been ousted by statute.[85] The substitute mechanisms for scrutiny of such matters have a largely formal overview jurisdiction, with little power to question in detail the substantive merits or legality of the exercise of these powers.[86]

The problem is not however confined to issues of national security. There is no general statutory or common law duty to provide reasons or supporting evidence across the full range of decisions taken by public administration. There are some specific statutory provisions applicable to a limited range of decision-making bodies,[87] and the one judicial attempt to create a general duty to give reasons[88] seems largely to be ignored by the administration and courts alike. Lastly, even at its most activist and penetrating level, judicial review is concerned with the legality, rationality (in a somewhat limited sense) and procedural propriety[89] of decisions taken by public administration. It is

---

81   See Wright, *Spycatcher*, for a description of the organisation and accountability of the security services.
82   Security Service Act 1988.
83   See, for example, *CCSU v Minister for Civil Service* [1985] AC 374 and *R v Home Secretary, Ex p. Hosenball* (above).
84   *Ponting* trial; Ponting, *op. cit.*
85   Interception of Communications Act 1985, section 9; Security Service Act 1988, Clause 5.
86   Interception of Communications Act 1985, sections 7 and 8; Security Service Act 1988, Schedule 1.
87   For example, Tribunals and Inquiries Act 1971, section 12.
88   *Padfield v Minister of Agriculture* [1968] AC 997.
89   *CCSU v Minister for Civil Service* [1984] 3 All ER 935, 950 to 951, per Lord Diplock.

only very exceptionally concerned with the substantive merits of those decisions, and will thus rarely require production of the full record or dossier of information upon the basis of which a decision has been taken. The formal process of discovery in litigation against public authorities whether by application for judicial review or by private law action is now highly restricted.[90]

Although the powers of the various ombudsmen to obtain information from public authorities, including central government, are considerably greater than those of the courts and parliament,[91] their jurisdiction is restricted to maladministration, which specifically excludes illegality and other grounds of review or appeal,[92] as well as the merits of discretionary decisions.[93] Furthermore, the ombudsmen may be expressly prohibited from revealing information obtained in the course of their investigations,[94] and at central government level, are bound by section 2 of the Official Secrets Act 1911.[95]

Lastly, although the new select committees have been able to extract considerably more information from central government over the past decade of their assistance and operation,[96] the Government has shown itself willing to defy the select committees in order to avoid revealing embarrassing information in a variety of areas, including housing,[97] defence and industrial policy.[98]

Given this weakness of the public law controls over the production of official information and the consequent power of government to prevent disclosure thereof it is disturbing that government should be able to resort to the private law to enhance the already considerable powers of government to maintain secrecy. The reform of section 2 of the Official Secrets Act 1911[99] will enhance government's power to prosecute third parties[100] who disclose information disclosed to them in consequence of an unlawful disclosure by a Crown servant or government contractor, with no defence of public interest or prior publication being available to such third parties.[101]

---

90 *Air Canada v Secretary of State for Trade* (above). RSC Ord. 53, r.8, provides for discovery on an application for judicial review, but leave must be obtained and is not automatic; see *O'Reilly v Mackman* [1982] 3 All ER 1124, 1132, per Lord Diplock.

91 Parliamentary Commissioner Act 1967, section 8; Local Government Act 1974, section 29.

92 Parliamentary Commissioner Act 1967, section 5(2); Local Government Act 1974, section 26(6).

93 Parliamentary Commissioner Act 1967, section 12(3); Local Government Act 1974, section 34(3).

94 Parliamentary Commissioner Act 1967, section 11; Local Government Act 1974, section 32.

95 Parliamentary Commissioner Act 1967, section 11.

96 See Davies, *Reformed Select Committees; The First Year*, OCPU, 1981; Drewry, 'Select Committees and Back-bench Power', in Jowell & Oliver (eds), *The Changing Constitution*, OUP, 2nd edn, 1989, Ch. 6.

97 Delbridge & Smith (eds) *Consuming Secrets*, Burnett Books, 1982, at 51 to 53.

98 Oliver & Austin, 'The Westland Affair' (1987) 40 *Parliamentary Affairs* 20.

99 Official Secrets Act 1989. See also White Paper on Reform of Section 2 of the Official Secrets Act 1911, Cmnd 408/1988.

100 Official Secrets Act 1989, section 5.

101 White Paper, Cmnd 408, above, paragraphs 58 to 64.

Newspapers and other publishers will thus be vulnerable to prosecution for publication of official information, even where they have no direct connection with the original wrongful disclosure. Again, given this considerable strengthening of the criminal law protecting official information, albeit concerning a substantially reduced range of subjects, it seems incongruous to permit government to resort to private law means to restrain publication of confidential information.

Conclusion

It has been shown that the Government has ample, indeed many would argue excessive, public law powers and administrative mechanisms to prevent and punish the disclosure of official information. The reduction of the areas covered by the Official Secrets Act 1911 will do little if anything to weaken the Government's powers, given the weakness, in practice, of the discredited section 2, the Government's indication that it intends to strengthen the civil service code of discipline[102] in respect of unauthorised disclosures and the extended application of the new provisions to third parties. The constitutional and legal controls over government in this area are notoriously weak.

For all these reasons, it is submitted that the freedom of the press in a democratic society to expose, in the public interest, the wrongdoings, inefficiency or incompetence of government and its agencies ought not to be further reduced by permitting government to resort to the inappropriate private law of confidence. If government is to be permitted, in exceptional circumstances, to exercise prior restraint over publication of sensitive official information, it should be by way of public law mechanisms with appropriate limitations and safeguards.

---

102   White Paper, Cmnd 408, above, paragraphs 71 to 73.

Parliament and the Press:
A Right to be Reported?

Dawn Oliver

Parliament and the press have long enjoyed a love-hate relationship. On many occasions in the last 300 years Parliament has invoked parliamentary privilege to deny the press the right to report its proceedings. Members of Parliament are naturally sensitive to criticism and each House has been careful of its reputation. And yet through the press Parliament may reach the public and communicate the legislature's central role in the country's political life (or on occasions its impotence). The relationship between these two institutions is inherently problematic.

Over the years there has been a number of notorious cases concerning publication of reports of the doings of Parliament in which publication has been found to be in breach of parliamentary privilege. In 1771 John Miller, a printer, was arrested and ordered to appear at the Bar of the House of Commons for printing reports of parliamentary debates, in breach of what was then the Commons' privilege not to have its proceedings published. Miller refused to appear before the House and had the House of Commons' messenger arrested and brought before the magistrates for assault and false imprisonment. The magistrates found that Miller had not been guilty of any offence and should not have been arrested, and therefore committed the messenger to prison for unlawfully arresting him. The House of Commons retaliated by committing the magistrates (the Lord Mayor of London, Aldermen Oliver MP and John Wilkes) to the Tower. They were released on the prorogation of Parliament, but meanwhile had been treated as heroes by the citizens of London, who were understandably hostile to attempts to suppress publication of Parliament's proceedings. The victory of the Commons against the courts and the press had been pyrrhic given the damage done to their reputation.

More recently in 1947 a journalist who was also a Member of Parliament, and his newspaper editor published 'unjustified' allegations in the *World's Press News* that Members of Parliament regularly betray the confidence of

Dawn Oliver, M.A. (Cantab.), Barrister, Senior Lecturer in Law at University College London

private party meetings either for payment or while their discretion has been undermined by drink: they were found to be in serious contempt of Parliament. The editor was summoned to the Bar of the House and reprimanded, and the Member of Parliament was expelled from the House.[1] In 1956 the editor of *The Sunday Graphic* was found to be in breach of parliamentary privilege when he published an article inviting readers to telephone a Member of Parliament at his home, giving his number, if they agreed with the newspaper that a question tabled by the Member was 'just about the most crazy, mixed-up question of the year'. The MP had been pestered by telephone calls as a result and had had to keep the phone off the hook and eventually had his telephone number changed.[2] The Committee of Privileges was of the view that this amounted to a serious breach of privilege resulting in the 'molestation' of the MP, but recommended that the apology of the editor be accepted and no further action be taken.

On the other hand there is clearly a strong interest on the part of the public in knowing what takes place in Parliament, and generally the press is the medium through which this may be communicated. The importance of this function of communication was recognised and strongly expressed by Lord Cockburn, Chief Justice in 1868 in the case of *Wason v Walter*.[3] This was an action for libel against one of the proprietors of *The Times* newspaper, for publishing a report of a debate in the House of Lords in which statements had been made reflecting on the plaintiff. The question was whether faithful and fair reports of proceedings in Parliament were 'privileged' in the sense that the reporting could not give rise to an action in defamation by anyone whose reputation was damaged by the report, as long as there was no malice in the reporting. Or should the press be prevented from publishing such reports? The Lord Chief Justice found for *The Times*. In this important judgment, which will be quoted at length, he sets out graphically the political rationale for the freedom to report on parliamentary proceedings:

It seems to us impossible to doubt that it is of paramount public and national importance that the proceedings of the houses of Parliament shall be communicated to the public, who have the deepest interest in knowing what passes within their walls, seeing that on what is there said and done the welfare of the community depends. Where would be our confidence in the Government of the country, or in the legislature by which our laws are framed, and to whose charge the great interests of the country are committed – where would be our attachment to the constitution under which we live, if the proceedings of the great council of the realm were shrouded in secrecy, and concealed from the knowledge of the nation? How could the communications between the representatives of the people and their constituents, which are so essential to the

---

1   *The Case of Garry Allighan MP.* Report from the Committee of Privileges (HC 138 of 1946 to 1947). Discussed in G. Wilson, *Cases and Materials in Constitutional and Administrative Law*, CUP, 1966, 1st edn, at 290 to 295.

2   *The Case of the Sunday Graphic*, First Report from the Committee of Privileges (HC 27 of 1956 to 1957), discussed in G. Wilson, *Cases and Materials in Constitutional and Administrative law*, CUP, 1966, 1st edn, at 287 to 289.

3   (1868) LR 4 QB 73.

working of the representative system, be usefully carried on if the constituencies were kept in ignorance of what their representatives are doing? What would become of the right of petitioning on all measures pending in Parliament, the undoubted right of the subject, if the people are to be kept in ignorance of what is passing in either house? Can any man bring himself to doubt that the publicity given in modern times to what passes in Parliament is essential to the maintenance of the relations subsisting between the government, the legislature and the country at large?[4]

It is noteworthy that this statement is put in terms of a general constitutional principle that the public should know what takes place in Parliament going far beyond the issue of defamation in that case.

The rationales for press freedom, particularly the freedom to report proceedings in Parliament, were eloquently stated in the judgment in *Wason v Walter*. Eric Barendt in *Freedom of Speech* considers a number of possible rationales for free speech and reaches a similar conclusion: 'The argument from democracy, that is the case that much political and social discussion should be immune from government suppression because it enables people to participate fully and knowledgeably in public affairs and to deal with government on a level of equality, is perhaps the most persuasive.'[5]

Although, as we have seen, Parliament has a history of seeking to prevent publication of its proceedings and comment upon them, there have, more recently, been times when Parliament has made the opposite claim, namely that it has a right to be reported. This was one of the issues raised by the *Spycatcher* litigation in 1987 and 1988. In one of these cases some members of the House of Commons took objection to attempts by the Government, operating through the courts, to deny it access to the public through the media.

The Spycatcher Injunction Against the BBC

The saga started in December 1987. The BBC was intending to broadcast the first of a series of programmes on Radio 4 entitled 'My Country: Right or Wrong' which was to be about the security services. The subject matter was covered by the sixth of the eight D-Notices, concerning British intelligence services.[6] Prior to the fixing of the date for the broadcast the BBC had secured approval from Admiral Higgins, Secretary of the D-Notice Committee. A number of distinguished politicians were to appear in the series,

---

4   Per Cockburn CJ in *Wason v Walter* (1868) LR 4 QB 73.

5   E. Barendt, *Freedom of Speech*, Oxford, Clarendon 1985, at 299.

6   For an account of the D-Notice system see Third Report from the Defence Committee, 1979 to 1980 HC 773, the D-Notice System; for the Government's response see *The D-Notice System: Observations presented by the Secretary of State for Defence*, Cmnd 8129, 1981. The Defence, Press and Broadcasting Committee then conducted a review of the system, outlined in Fourth Report from the Defence Committee 1982 to 1983: Previous Recommendations of the Committee (1982 to 1983 HC 55) at xi to xii. See generally S.H. Bailey, D.J. Harris and B.L. Jones, *Civil Liberties: Cases and Materials*, Butterworths, 2nd edn, 1985, at 328 to 333.

including Admiral Higgins. It was no secret that the series was planned, and Admiral Higgins, having been given a summary of the content of the programme, was satisfied that there were nothing in it to damage national security.

On 4 December the Attorney-General applied to the High Court for an interlocutory injunction preventing the BBC from transmitting the programme until the trial, when the substantive issues could be resolved. The Attorney-General's objection was founded on fears for national security, and public confidence in, and the morale of, the security services. At that time, it will be remembered, the *Spycatcher* case was part heard. One of the issues in that case was the apparent inconsistency in the Government's approach to publication of matters relating to security. No steps had been taken to suppress publication of Chapman Pincher's book *Their Trade is Treachery*. It seemed that the Attorney-General's application for an injunction against the BBC had as part of its rationale the desire to establish a consistent approach by the Government in these matters.

The injunction granted to the Attorney-General was in very broad terms. It prevented the BBC from broadcasting 'any interviews with, or information derived from, current or former members of the security or intelligence services of the United Kingdom relating to any aspect of the work of the said services, including their identity as current or former members thereof'.[7] The injunction was not, therefore, restricted to broadcasting of the programme 'My Country: Right or Wrong', nor to information that was confidential or potentially damaging to national security. On the face of it these terms would also cover reports of court or parliamentary proceedings in which the security services were mentioned. Further, as a result of the *Spycatcher* decision, *AG v Newspaper Publishing plc*,[8] the injunction would be binding not only on the BBC, but also on other broadcasting organisations and possibly even on other media who might publish such information knowing that it was subject to a pending action and the subject of a court order prohibiting its publication.

The implications of this injunction were quickly seized upon by the media and by Members of Parliament. The order was yet another example of the Government seeking and the courts granting prior restraint on publication (something which is forbidden in many countries, notably the United States,[9] by the Constitution) and of a drastic use of civil proceedings to protect confidential information. These issues were raised repeatedly in the *Spycatcher* litigation, which is considered by other papers in this volume.

In addition to the large number of cases involving *Spycatcher* there have been numerous examples in the last few years of the Government seeking to

---

7   *The Independent* 8 December 1987.
8   [1987] 3 WLR 942.
9   See the Constitution of the United States of America, First Amendment: 'Congress shall make no law . . . abridging the freedom of speech, or of the press'.

prevent or punish publication or broadcasting of material which poses no real security risk but is embarrassing to the Government or offensive to some sections of the public. The Home Secretary's ban in November 1988 on broadcasting of interviews with terrorist organisations in Ireland is but one example. Others include the *Ponting* case and the prosecution of Sarah Tisdall for disclosing unauthorized information carrying no security risk; in addition the Government put pressure on the BBC in July 1985 not to broadcast 'Real Lives', a programme about the IRA and Northern Ireland; and in January 1987 the Government pressed the BBC to withdraw the series 'Secret Society' which disclosed the concealment of expenditure on a UK intelligence satellite, code-named *Zircon*; this particular incident culminated in the police seizure of the tapes (the programme was eventually broadcast in September 1988).[10]

Against this background of government suppression of information the freedom of speech in Parliament that is guaranteed by Article 9 of the Bill of Rights 1688 and the reporting of proceedings in Parliament may be seen to be particularly important as safeguards against abuse of power by state organisations such as the security services or ministers. The possibility of attempts on the part of government to suppress even reports of parliamentary or judicial proceedings is a real one: in March/April 1989 an injunction was granted on the application of the Secretary of State for Trade and Industry, Lord Young, restraining publication of a special issue of *The Observer*, which contained reports on the content of a Department of Trade and Industry report on the Harrods takeover, and restraining also all publication of the contents of this report. The injunction was later amended to exclude from the restriction reports on parliamentary or judicial proceedings. So one important issue raised by the *Spycatcher* injunction which attracted a good deal of controversy and comment in the House of Commons at the time was whether the injunction might represent a breach of parliamentary privilege if it prevented the BBC − and other media − from broadcasting or reporting on parliamentary discussion of the security services or the BBC series or the granting of the injunction.

The issue was a transitory one in the House of Commons because on 9 December 1987 the Attorney-General agreed at a meeting in chambers before Owen J with the BBC that the terms of the injunction should be modified so as to permit 'fair and accurate' reports of proceedings in Parliament and in the courts. Whether the offer was made in the belief that the Government did indeed run the risk of being in contempt of Parliament, or whether their reasons were to do with public relations or others is not known. The BBC could, under this agreement, refer to security matters and the names of former or present agents, but only if the information had been mentioned in Parliament or in proceedings in open court and had already been made public 'with the authority of the Crown'.[11]

---

10   For an account of this trend towards prior restraint see vol. 19, *Index on Censorship*, September 1988.
11   See *The Independent* 10 December 1987.

Thereafter interest in this issue died down, but nevertheless it raises interesting points about Parliament's access to the media and the freedom of the press.

The matter of breach of privilege was raised in the House on 7 December 1987 by a number of MPs. They seemed to be assuming that the injunction, or any attempt to commit the BBC for contempt for reporting on the proceedings of the House would constitute 'a serious infringement of our rights'.[12] Tony Banks MP asked the Speaker:

Can you assure the House that any matter that is raised in the House in relation to the BBC's position regarding the injunction and the programme 'My Country: Right or Wrong' can be reported by the BBC, because anything that is said here is, of course, covered by parliamentary privilege? In fact, I understand that the terms of the injunction seem to be preventing the BBC from even reporting the proceedings of the House. Clearly there must be a serious infringement of our rights.[13]

The Speaker replied, somewhat opaquely, that 'The Hon. Member knows that anything that is mentioned in the House is in the public domain. It is a matter for the BBC whether it reports what is said.'[14]

Mr Frank Dobson attempted to clarify this statement by asking:

Will you confirm that if it is in the public domain, if the BBC reports it and if any action is taken by the Government following that reporting, you would regard that action by the Government as a gross contempt of this High Court of Parliament?[15]

Mr John Morris, the shadow Attorney-General, maintained that:

It would be a grave incursion into the liberties of the House if action were taken against anyone who reported the proceedings of the House in that way.[16]

It seems therefore that these MPs were asserting that it is part of the privilege of Parliament to be reported in the media. The question arises, is there any warrant for this view, and what does it tell us about Parliament and parliamentary privilege?

At first sight the claim seems to be quite inconsistent with all notions of parliamentary privilege. Privilege is designed to protect the House and its members and officials from civil and criminal proceedings that might interfere with their parliamentary duties, and to protect Parliament's independence and reputation. Privilege is not designed to protect others, such as the BBC, from civil or criminal proceedings. As Blackstone put it in his *Commentaries on the Laws of England*:

Privilege of Parliament was principally established in order to protect its members not only from being molested by their fellow-subjects, but also and more especially from being oppressed by the power of the Crown.[17]

---

12   Tony Banks, HC Deb. 1987 to 1988, 7 Dec. col. 22.
13   *Ibid*.
14   *Ibid*.
15   HC Deb. 1987 to 1988, 7 Dec. col. 24.
16   *Ibid*.
17   Vol. I, at 163.

This was not, however, how the MPs who raised the issue saw it. Mr Dennis Skinner MP developed that argument as follows:

The BBC was given the power and right by the House to record the proceedings of the House of Commons, provided it was done in a fair and responsible and balanced way. However, as a result of the injunction the reporting could not be balanced. And it is therefore the duty of the Speaker and the House to see that the BBC's remit is carried out.[18]

The Speaker's response, not surprisingly, was that 'It has never been the responsibility of the Speaker to decide which parts of our proceedings should be broadcast.'[19]

The History of the Parliamentary Privilege of Free Speech and the Right to Control Publication of Proceedings

The question of publication of parliamentary proceedings which was in issue in the BBC case is bound up with freedom of speech in Parliament. Privilege was originally claimed in order to protect members of both Houses of Parliament from the King and their constituents and to uphold the dignity and proper functioning of Parliament. Strode's Act of 1512 provided that 'all suits, etc. against all persons of that particular or any other Parliament . . . for any Bill, or speaking of any matter concerning the Parliament be of none effect'. The Act was passed in response to the imprisonment of Richard Strode by a court for having introduced a bill in Parliament to regulate the tin industry. It sought to prevent the harassment of MPs by aggrieved citizens through the courts.

Freedom of speech in Parliament was regularly claimed by Sir Thomas More, as Speaker, from Henry VIII, but it was not regarded as a matter of right at that period. From the early reign of Elizabeth I free speech was claimed as a matter of right (although the Queen did not invariably respect it).

The right to free speech was eventually conceded by the Crown after the *Case of the Three Members* (*R v Eliot, Hollis and Valentine*[20]). Three MPs had been imprisoned and fined by the Court of King's Bench in 1629 at the

---

18 The implication of this view would seem to be that the BBC itself would be in breach of privilege if it did not report in a balanced way. It is clear that the House of Commons has the power to revoke its resolution granting to the BBC the right to broadcast its proceedings. If unbalanced reporting were to bring the House into disrepute, then the BBC would be liable to be treated as in contempt of Parliament. See generally S.A. de Smith, *Constitutional and Administrative Law*, Pelican Books, 5th edn, ch. 16; E.C.S. Wade and A.W. Bradley, *Constitutional and Administrative Law*, Longman, 10th edn, chapter 12.
19 Col.26.
20 3 St.Tr. 294; see Taswell-Langmead, *Constitutional History*, Sweet and Maxwell, 11th edn, 1960, at 377 to 378, 390.

behest of the King for seditious words spoken in the House. Parliament passed resolutions against this judgment in 1641 and 1667 and it was finally reversed by a writ of error by the Lords in 1668. Since that year the Crown has not taken legal proceedings against members for words spoken in the Parliament. Article Nine of the Bill of Rights 1688 declared that 'freedom of speech and debates or proceedings in Parliament ought not to be impeached or questioned in any Court or place outside of Parliament'; this measure seems to put freedom of speech beyond doubt.

The House's claim to be entitled to restrain publication of reports of proceedings in Parliament was originally a corollary of the privilege of freedom of speech. The publication of parliamentary debates was forbidden by Parliament in the seventeenth century. The rationale for this privilege against publication was that privacy might be necessary to secure freedom of debate.[21] It was regarded as essential in order to protect MPs from the Crown, as the monarchy had a record in the *Case of the Three Members*, 1629 (discussed above) and in other cases of arresting MPs who made speeches and comments of which the King disapproved. Later the privilege to restrain publication of parliamentary proceedings was claimed to be justified by the need to protect MPs from their constituents. This justification was soon recognised as being anti-democratic after the *John Miller* case in 1771 (above), although it surfaced again in the case of *The Sunday Graphic* referred to earlier.[22] After the *John Miller* case the Commons, though they continued to claim to treat publication of their proceedings as a breach of privilege until 1971, ceased to enforce this restriction save in exceptional circumstances.[23]

Parliament's Attitude to Publication Changes

Since the early 1800s Parliament has reversed its attitude to publication and has given positive encouragement to the publication of its proceedings. After the Reform Act 1832, reporters' galleries were provided in the House of Commons.[24] Hansard, the unofficial reports of parliamentary debates, began to be publishd in 1803, and the official publication, the House of Commons Debates, has been published since 1909. (Though known as 'Hansard' they

---

21   Erskine May, *Parliamentary Practice*, 20th edn, at 83. A similar argument is put forward for secrecy of Cabinet discussions: see *AG v Jonathan Cape* [1976] QB 752.

22   First Report from the Committee of Privileges (HC 27 of 1956 to 1957).

23   During the First and Second World Wars the House of Commons resolved from time to time to hold 'secret sessions'. But the Speaker published reports of these discussions, exercising discretion as to how much information the report contained about the confidential matters discussed. And on 19 December 1945 it was resolved that no proceedings during the last Parliament held in secret be any longer secret.

24   See O. Hood Phillips, *Constitutional and Administrative Law*, Sweet and Maxwell, 6th edn, 1978, at 239 to 240.

are no longer connected with the family firm that produced the original unofficial reports.) In 1971 the Commons resolved that: '. . . this House will not entertain any complaint of contempt of the House or breach of privilege in respect of the publication of the debates or proceedings of the House or of its Committees, except when any such debates or proceedings shall have been conducted with closed doors or in private or when such publication shall have been expressly prohibited by the House.'[25]

Since 1978 broadcasting from both Houses of Parliament has been authorised by resolutions; the only methods by which broadcasting may be prevented is by a decision of the House to exclude strangers, or by a direction from the Select Committee responsible for broadcasting.

Not only did publishers of reports of parliamentary proceedings originally risk being found in contempt of Parliament, but they also risked being sued for defamation if they reported any defamatory statements made in Parliament or if they published parliamentary papers containing defamatory material. Strode's Act protected only MPs. This latter risk was nullified by the Parliamentary Papers Act 1840. This measure gives publishers immunity from civil or criminal proceedings for the publication of material printed by order of the House, and for publication of any extract from or abstract of reports and proceedings.[26] It is noteworthy that the protection is not limited to defamation. The Parliamentary Papers Act does not, however, protect comment or publication in a form other than an extract or abstract.[27] The 1840 Act was extended to publication by broadcasting by the Defamation Act 1952, section 9. The Act also protects the publishers of a correct copy of an authorised paper, report, etc.

As far as reports of parliamentary proceedings are concerned, the defence of 'qualified privilege' in defamation actions extends to fair and accurate reports of parliamentary proceedings;[28] and comment is protected in the law of defamation by qualified privilege provided it is fair and honest and made without malice. The rationale for this rule, the public's need to know what takes place in Parliament, was strongly stated by Cockburn CJ in *Wason v Walter*,[29] quoted earlier in this essay.

To return to the *Spycatcher* injunction, the press and the broadcasting media would have been free, but for the injunction, to report on any discussion in Parliament of the case without running the risk of defamation actions (for example at the suit of Wright). Further, they could, under the Parliamentary Papers Act 1840, section 3, carry a verbatim extract from parliamentary

---

25 Erskine May, *Parliamentary Practice*, at 83.
26 Section 3 of this Act provides that '. . . it shall be lawful in any civil or criminal proceedings to be commenced or prosecuted for printing any extract from or abstract of such report, paper, votes, or proceedings to show that such extract or abstract was published bona fide and without malice . . .'
27 Erskine May, *Parliamentary Practice*, at 88.
28 Defamation Act 1952, section 7. *Beech v Freeson* [1971] 2 All ER 805.
29 (1868) LR 4 QB 73.

proceedings or an abstract without being liable in any civil or criminal proceedings, including proceedings for disclosing confidential information or for breach of the Official Secrets Act 1911. Both members of Parliament and the press have this defence to publication.[30] It seems, therefore, that the Attorney-General had no grounds for obtaining an injunction restraining the BBC from broadcasting extracts or abstracts of proceedings in Parliament in the absence of bad faith or malice. The BBC's case on this matter rested not on parliamentary privilege, as claimed by the MPs who complained to the Speaker, but on the defence provided by the 1840 Act. That 1840 Act does not, however, cover comment or anything other than verbatim extracts or abstracts, and here, it seems, the court would have had jurisdiction to make an order preventing editorial comment without laying themselves open to a charge of breach of parliamentary privilege or contempt of Parliament. Whether the court exercised its discretion to make such an order properly is another matter to which we shall return.

At one time the extent of parliamentary privilege was unclear. Privileges have never been codified. Blackstone in his *Commentaries on the Laws of England*, 1825, saw this as a positive advantage:

If therefore all the privileges of Parliament were once to be set down and ascertained, and no privilege to be allowed but what was so defined and determined, it were easy for the executive power to devise some new case, not within the line of privilege, and under pretence thereof to harass any refractory member and violate the freedom of Parliament.[31]

However, the courts have assumed the jurisdiction (disputed by Parliament)[32] to determine whether a privilege claimed by Parliament exists, though once satisfied that it does a judge will not review the manner of its exercise[33]: privilege is enforced by the House, not by the courts.

In 1704 both Houses resolved that they could not create new privileges not warranted by the known law and customs of Parliament.[34] The House of Commons resolved in 1978 that it should not extend its privileges or invoke them unless to do so was essential to enable the House to carry on its business.[35] The House should not, it was felt, be over-sensitive to criticism

---

30   In the *Duncan Sandys* case the House decided that Members are privileged from prosecution under the Official Secrets Act 1911 for disclosures made in the House, and they may not be required to divulge in a court of inquiry the sources of secret information used by them to frame questions in the House, although they should use their immunity with discretion (1938) HC Pap. 173; (1939) HC Pap. 101.
31   *Commentaries*, vol. I, at 163.
32   See the case history of *Ashby v White* 2 Ld. Raym. 938, 3 Ld. Raym. 320; 14 St.Tr. 695; and *Paty's* case Ld. Raym. 1105. See De Smith *Constitutional and Administrative Law*, Pelican Books, 5th edn, at 339 to 343.
33   *Bradlaugh v Gossett* (1884) 12 QBD 271.
34   Erskine May, *Parliamentary Practice*, at 75.
35   943 HC Deb. at 1155 to 1198 (6 February 1978).

and pressure. Clearly therefore neither House can extend its privileges, save by legislation. The courts take the same view.[36]

But one question that arises out of the BBC case is whether the House of Commons has the power to *extend* its privileges to meet new challenges to its ability to perform its functions and to its independence. Ought the House to be in a position to charge the Attorney-General with breach of privilege or contempt of Parliament when he seeks to prevent the BBC from fulfilling its duty to give a balanced picture of Parliament through its broadcasting of proceedings, as claimed by Mr Dennis Skinner MP, even though this has not been a breach of privilege on past decision? Ought Parliament to have a right to be reported without interference by the courts at the behest of the Attorney-General or any other litigant?

The New View of Parliament's Role

It will be seen that over a period of some 200 years the attitude of the House of Commons to the publication and reporting of and commentary on its proceedings has altered dramatically, from a fierce protection of *a right not to be reported* to, in the 'My Country: Right or Wrong' case, a claim from some quarters *to be entitled to be reported* (at least by the BBC with its obligation to ensure political balance in its reporting).

It is clear, however, that parliamentary privilege has never extended to giving a publisher a right to report on parliamentary proceedings. At most Parliament may be said to have surrendered its own claim to be entitled to prevent such publication, leaving would-be publishers with their common law freedom to publish and the protection of privilege in defamation actions (which is quite separate from parliamentary privilege) unless some other rule of common law or some statutory provision prevents such publication. Hence there was clearly no foundation for the complaints by Members of Parliament in relation to the *Spycatcher* injunction that prevention of reports of parliamentary proceedings amounted to a breach of parliamentary privilege. And the time is long passed where either House could assert a new privilege, except by legislation. However it does seem that the injunction in *Spycatcher* restraining publication of verbatim extracts or abstracts of parliamentary proceedings was made without jurisdiction, because of section 3 of the Parliamentary Papers Act 1840.

Nevertheless the members of Parliament who complained about the terms of the *Spycatcher* injunction of 4 December 1987 clearly had an important constitutional point to make, and a point that has been recognised by the courts, as the Lord Chief Justice's comments as long ago as 1868 in *Wason*

---

36   See *Stockdale v Hansard* (1839) 3 A and E 1; 3 St.Tr. (NS) 723; *re Parliamentary Privilege Act 1770* [1958] AC 331; *Stourton v Stourton* [1963] P 302.

v Walter indicate. When injunctions are sought which restrain the reporting of parliamentary proceedings it is important that the courts should weigh up the constitutional issues against other public interests, such as national security. In principle, it is suggested, the discretion to grant injunctions that override the force of the constitutional principle set out by Cockburn CJ in *Wason v Walter* should be exercised extremely sparingly where the effect of the injunction is to immunise public bodies from any kind of legal or political accountability for their exercise of power.

Government, Parliament, the Public and the Press

This *Spycatcher* injunction case and the reactions of some MPs to it is interesting in highlighting the changed relationships between MPs, the Government and the public and the role of the press and other media in respect of these relationships.

It is no longer regarded as necessary to protect MPs from the executive by preventing publication of parliamentary proceedings. Indeed, with a parliamentary executive it would be futile to seek to do so. Nor is it regarded as appropriate to protect MPs from their constituents in this way. Quite the reverse, as the judgment in *Wason v Walter* quoted above indicates, it is now seen to be essential that members of the public should know both what their MPs do and say in Parliament, and what the government of the day is saying and doing (subject of course to some restrictions, especially in the area of national security).

Before the development of effective mass communications through the press and broadcasting media the Member of Parliament was the principal constitutional channel for communication between constituents and the King or government. The MP and his virtual monopoly of this communication channel was essential to the role of Parliament as the 'great council of the realm' and its function in insisting on redress of grievance before the granting of supply. The jealousy with which MPs claimed this role as exclusively theirs and denied it to the press indicates how important it was seen to be.[37]

Nowadays however the press and broadcasting media provide a means whereby the public can communicate directly to the Government without resort to MPs as intermediaries; and a means whereby the Government may communicate directly to the public, again without going through Parliament. The authorisation of the broadcasting of House of Commons proceedings indicates the desire of the House to be a part of the direct communication with the public which dominates modern politics. We may therefore see the claims

---

37   To an extent the role is still jealously guarded by MPs, for example in their insistence that complaints or grievances addressed to the Parliamentary Commissioner for Administration (the 'Ombudsman') should be channelled through the complainant's MP.

of members of Parliament to be entitled to be reported in the press as evidence of a wish to break into this communication system that enables the public and government to bypass Parliament. It also gave expression to an important constitutional principle of accountability.

It is clear nevertheless that the relationship between Parliament and the press remains delicate. The Members concerned about *Spycatcher* were anxious to continue to have access to the public via the BBC. It is questionable whether they would have reacted in the same way to injunctions granted against more polemical, partisan media institutions or reporting.

Do Broadcasters Need Free Speech?

Alan E. Boyle

This essay is about how the role of broadcasting in providing information and debate on matters of political controversy and public interest will fare under policies and proposals put forward by Mrs Thatcher's Government. It makes the obvious point that what we see and hear on broadcast media is determined largely by how those media are structured and regulated, and the less obvious point that, in broadcasting, the protection of free speech does not guarantee the provision of speech on matters of public interest. Viewed in historical terms, British broadcasting is at the threshold of a fundamental change in its organising philosophy, a change engineered by government for purposes still dimly perceived, but whose effect will be to move British broadcasting away from its public service tradition and towards a free speech-free market orientation.

The reasons for this radical shift in philosophy are only partly explained by government hostility to broadcasting on political and controversial issues. In itself such hostility is nothing new, and by no means the prerogative of Mrs Thatcher. During the General Strike of 1926, the BBC's coverage of events caused a brief ban on broadcasting 'matters of political, religious or industrial controversy.'[1] At the time of the Suez Crisis in 1956, the Prime Minister allegedly threatened a government takeover of the BBC.[2] Harold Wilson's distaste for the BBC during his prime ministership is well documented and his appointment of Lord Hill of Luton as its chairman was widely seen as an attempt to tame the Corporation.[3]

The present Government has been vociferous in its criticism of certain aspects of BBC and IBA broadcasting. The former has offended by its even-handedness during the Falklands War, and by its honesty in reporting civilian

Alan E. Boyle, M.A., B.C.L.(Oxon.) Barrister, Lecturer, Faculty of Law, Queen Mary and Westfield College, University of London

1   Report of the Committee on the Future of Broadcasting (the Annan Report) Cmnd 6753 (1977) paragraph 5.10. The ban was lifted in 1928.
2   Munro, *Television, Censorship and the Law*, Saxon House, 1979, at 13.
3   Munro, at 18.

casualties of US air raids on Libya. The attempted suppression of its documentary on extremist politicians in Northern Ireland ended in the departure of the Director-General and the Home Secretary.[4] Most remarkable of all have been the police raids on BBC offices and the seizure of programme material allegedly relating to a secret spy satellite. The IBA has incurred ministerial displeasure for its approval of the documentary 'Death on the Rock', which made allegations about the conduct of British soldiers in killing suspected terrorists.

One response to this history of friction is simply to say that it indicates the BBC and IBA are doing their jobs well. They were set up as public services, to inform and to educate, and the evidence of distressed politicians of all parties is a clear sign that they do facilitate pointed debate on matters of public interest. That is certainly what we have come to expect of them.[5] The range, diversity and authority of the BBC's coverage of public affairs on radio and television is simply unequalled by any other broadcasting system elsewhere, and it is strongly complemented by the present commercial channels. The contribution of both systems to informing the electorate and ensuring a real discussion of public affairs is a point politicians are right to recognise.[6] Equally, few other systems, including the American, expose national politicians and their policies to such searching inquiry or such homely but revealing insights.

But what gives Mrs Thatcher's relationship with the BBC and IBA a qualitative difference from any preceding administration is her Government's willingness to question the role of public broadcasting, not on its performance, but on ideological grounds. Both broadcasting institutions sit uneasily beside a philosophy of withdrawing the state from public life and allowing greater competition and a free market to prevail. Applied to broadcasting, this puts at risk not only the BBC and IBA themselves, but the whole concept of public service broadcasting, as it has traditionally been applied across the spectrum in Britain.

Departures from the public service model have already been sanctioned in the case of cable and satellite services.[7] If the market-oriented approach of the Peacock Report[8] and the Government's 1988 White Paper[9] become the basis for all future broadcasting, what then will protect the media's role as providers of informed, independent commentary on public affairs? Is that role, and its effective performance, a product of the public service regulation we

---

4   See Boyle (1986) PL 562 at 571 and *The Times* 6 and 7 August 1985.
5   For accounts of the development of broadcasting on political issues in Britain, see Goldie, *Facing the Nation*, Bodley Head, 1977, and Sendall, *Independent Television in Britain*, 3 vols, Macmillan 1982.
6   See Blumler and McQuail, *Television in Politics: Its Uses and Influence*, Faber 1968; Smith, *Television and Political Life*, Macmillan 1979, ch. 1.
7   Cable and Broadcasting Act 1984.
8   *Report of the Committee on Financing the BBC* Cmnd 9824 (1986). On radio deregulation see *Radio: Choice and Opportunities* Cm 92 (1987), noted (1988) PL 24.
9   *Broadcasting in the 1990s: Competition, Choice and Quality*, Cm. 517 (1988).

now have? Or can free speech – the absence of governmental regulation in a free market – work for broadcasting as it has for the press, and continue to provide us with the level and quality of service hitherto enjoyed?

These are fundamental choices, and they go to the heart of the question as to what kind of broadcasting we want. The central assumption of this chapter is that a structure for broadcasting which leaves us with little or no coverage of political issues, or coverage so one-sided that, like *The Sun*, it serves no purpose, presents serious dangers to our political culture, and should be avoided if we value the reality of free speech and informed debate, and not its empty form.

Politics and the Public Service Concept of Broadcasting

The concept of broadcasting as a public service is the main feature of the BBC's Charter[10] and the legislation governing IBA television and radio.[11] It serves two functions, creating both expectations and restraints. Expectation, because it defines the kind of service the broadcasting organisations must provide, and thus has a direct impact on the style and content of their programmes. Restraint, because it inhibits direct government interference with their pro-gramming. Having defined broadcasting standards in advance, governments cannot then use their power to demand something else.

Public service broadcasting has at least four significant characteristics: it involves restrictions on content, limited freedom of speech for the broad-casting bodies themselves, guaranteed access for political parties in certain circumstances, and a system of accountability for the fulfilment of these obligations.[12] Content is controlled in a number of ways. Services of a high standard must be provided, with a proper balance and a wide range in subject matter, including accurate and impartial news broadcasts.[13] The IBA is required by statute,[14] and the BBC by implication, to serve the needs of information, education and entertainment. Thus neither body can avoid the presentation of political issues or take refuge in entertainment alone if they are to do their job, a point accepted by the Committee whose report preceded establishment of the BBC in 1925.[15]

Within this range, programme content is further defined. Requirements of taste, decency, impartiality, balance, public order and in the case of news,

---

10 Cmnd 8313 (1981). The licence is Cmnd 8233 (1981).
11 Broadcasting Act 1981; Licence Cmnd 6467 (1981).
12 See generally, Munro, *Television, Censorship, and the Law*; Boyle, (1986) PL 562.
13 Resolution of BBC Board of Governors, 8 January 1981, annexed to the licence of 1981, Cmnd 8233; Broadcasting Act 1981 sections 2(2), 4, and 11(2); *Wilson v IBA* (1979) SC 351.
14 Broadcasting Act 1981, section 2(2).
15 *Report of the Broadcasting Committee* (1925) Cmnd 2599.

accuracy, must be met.[16] What these criteria mean is itself far from clear, and open in practice to broad and varied judgments.[17] But their implications for political coverage include fair treatment of parliamentary parties and political issues.[18] There is no freedom to be one-sided.

Two features indicate how the public service concept of broadcasting is in important respects the antithesis of the kind of free speech enjoyed by newspapers. The broadcasting bodies may not themselves offer editorial judgments on public issues:[19] unlike the press they cannot seek directly to influence the political views of their audience. Conversely, direct access for precisely that purpose is essentially guaranteed to political parties and government. This is not a product of the charter or the legislation. Instead, it rests on undertakings given by both organisations and formalised by long practice.[20] As a result, ministerial, party political and election broadcasts obtain free air time, allocated on a basis supposedly faithful to the requirements of fairness, and including where appropriate some rights of reply.[21] The corollary is that no political advertising is permitted:[22] the purchase of broadcasting space which helps make American elections so expensive, and favours those with the deepest pocket, is thus entirely avoided, but in effect, the broadcasters are forced instead to carry programmes they might otherwise wish to avoid. In this very precise way, broadcasting has been given a functional role as a platform in the democratic process.

The final feature is accountability. For both BBC and IBA, this is a complex and somewhat diffuse mixture of institutional, governmental, parliamentary and judicial controls. There is even, since 1980, a Broadcasting Complaints Commission,[23] and now a Broadcasting Standards Council.[24] Accountability is meant to ensure that broadcasters comply with the policy laid down for them.[25] The obvious danger, however, is of letting government, or the courts, under the guise of accountability, assume the role of censor. That is not how the system is designed to operate, nor does it often do so in practice, but, as the recent ban on interviews with members of Sinn Fein indicates,[26] there are exceptions to this.

---

16   Resolution of Board of Governors of the BBC, 8 January 1981, annexed to the licence, Cmnd 8233; Broadcasting Act 1981, sections 2(2), 4.
17   See *Att. Gen. ex rel McWhirter v IBA* (1973) QB 629; *McAliskey v BBC* (1980) NI 44; *Lynch v BBC* [1983] 6 NIJB 1; *Wilson v IBA* (1979) SC 351; *Wilson v IBA* (1988) SLT 276.
18   Boyle, at 572 to 587.
19   BBC licence, paragraph 13(7); Broadcasting Act 1981, section 4(2).
20   *Aide-memoire* of 1947, Cmnd 8117; *Aide-memoire* of 1969, reproduced in Goldie, at 343. See Annan Report, paragraphs 18 to 20.
21   These requirements have not been free of controversy; *R v Broadcasting Complaints Commission, ex parte Owen* [1985] QB 1153; Boyle, (1987) 8 J Media L 6.
22   BBC licence, paragraph 12; Broadcasting Act 1981, Schedule 2, paragraph 8.
23   Broadcasting Act 1981, sections 53 to 60; *R v Broadcasting Complaints Commission ex parte Owen* [1985] QB 1153.
24   The 1988 White Paper proposes that this body will be given a statutory responsibility to monitor sex and violence in programming.
25   See Boyle, (1986) PL 562.
26   See *The Independent*, 21 October 1988.

The Board of Governors of the BBC, and the Board of the IBA, are primarily responsible for ensuring that what is broadcast conforms to the required standards.[27] In that sense, they are the censors, not government or the courts.[28] The role of Parliament, and government, is confined in principle to matters of broadcasting policy. Parliament acts through legislation and periodic reviews of broadcasting performance, such as the Annan Report on the Future of Broadcasting. Ultimately, it is to it that the broadcasting organisations must answer. Parliament's role is ensured by the need for periodic renewal of the BBC Charter and the IBA's statutory mandate, and by setting the level of BBC income through the licence fee.[29]

Government can exercise further control by giving directions on broadcasting policy.[30] This is provided for in the BBC licence and the legislation, and includes the right for the Home Secretary to prohibit broadcasts on any matter or classes of matters, and to control the time of broadcasting.[31] Though apparently extensive, such powers have been rarely used, and there is a strong convention that despite their width, they must not be invoked to interfere with specific programmes.[32] Nevertheless, by retaining the right to set limits as a matter of policy, the Government possesses an important power of potential censorship.

The role of the courts in exercising judicial review of the broadcasting boards is more limited. There have been few successful challenges to programming decisions and the courts are reluctant to substitute their own judgment on subjective issues of taste, decency, balance or impartiality.[33] But they do have an important role in making the broadcasters define their standards, as happened when the SDP challenged the impartiality and balance of BBC coverage of their party, and in providing a forum for adjudicating on such disputes.[34] This serves to reinforce the broadcaster's obedience to the rules but it also helps them resist politicians who might wish to deflect them from their standards. The court's main value is thus as independent arbiters free of the limitations of political accountability.

Accountable to other institutions, unlike the press, the broadcasting bodies are therefore not fully independent, despite the fact that neither is part of the

---

27   See Paulu, *Television and Radio in the UK*, Macmillan, 1981, chapters 3 and 5; Smith, above, Note 6; Goldie, chapter 13; Munro, chapters 6 and 7.

28   *Att. Gen. ex rel McWhirter v IBA* [1973] QB 629; *R v IBA ex parte Whitehouse, The Times*, 4 April 1985.

29   Munro, chapters 2 and 3; Paulu, at 109 to 112; Smith, above, Note 6; The Peacock Report, above, Note 8, at paragraph 2.4.

30   Annan Report, chapter 5.

31   BBC Licence, clauses 13(4), 14(1); Broadcasting Act 1981, sections 28, 29(3); these powers were used for the October 1988 ban on interviews with members of terrorist groups in Northern Ireland, above, Note 26.

32   Annan Report, chapter 5.

33   *Att. Gen. ex rel McWhirter v IBA* [1973] QB 629; *McAliskey v BBC* [1980] NI 44; *Lynch v BBC* [1983] 6 NIJBI; *R v IBA ex parte Whitehouse, The Times*, 4 April 1985; *R v Broadcasting Complaints Commission ex parte Owen* [1985] QB 1153.

34   Boyle, at 592 to 596.

Crown,[35] and that the BBC was created as a corporation to emphasise its separation from government influence.[36] This lack of full autonomy must not be over-emphasised however. The practical independence of the broadcasting bodies in what they show is very great: few Home Secretaries would wish to repeat Leon Brittan's mistake of trying publicly to have a programme stopped by the BBC Governors.[37]

That practical independence from government is protected in part by Parliamentary vigilance, in part by the courts, but mostly by those who have directed the BBC and IBA and upheld the standards they are meant to serve. The subtle combination of public ownership or control, with public service standards of programming, has thus avoided both private monopoly power, and political subservience to those in government. Measured in freedom of debate, it has worked. How, by comparison, would a free speech or free market solution fare?

A Free Market in Broadcasting? The American System in Operation

American broadcasting developed differently from the British model. The same assumptions about scarcity of frequencies, and evidence of chaotic competition among those available in the 1920s were used to justify regulation, at least to the extent of allocating available channels.[38] Once decisions on who should be licensed had to be made, it was inevitable that the content of what was broadcast would become an important criterion. Thus, through its licensing function, the Federal Communications Commission (FCC) became the body which could determine policy on such issues as quality, diversity, balance and fairness. Its statutory mandate allowed it to act on grounds of 'public interest, convenience or necessity' and to enforce its rules, if necessary, by orders and licence revocation.[39]

This clearly did not give broadcasters free speech, in the sense that newspapers enjoyed that freedom.[40] Yet neither did it result in a full public service system like the British. Uncomfortable with the notion of a state owned public broadcasting service, the philosophy of the US approach has fallen between two stools. Most importantly there has been no BBC; the Public Broadcasting System,[41] which today supplies much of the quality broadcasting and the

---

35   *BBC v Johns* [1965] Ch. 32.

36   *Report of the Broadcasting Committee*, (1925) Cmnd 2599, paragraphs 5, 16.

37   See Note 4, above.

38   *National Broadcasting Co. v US* 319 US 190 (1943); *Red Lion Broadcasting Co. v FCC* 395 US 367 (1969).

39   The Communications Act 1934; 47 USC.

40   *Red Lion Broadcasting Co. v FCC* 395 US 367 (1969); *CBS v Democratic National Committee* 412 US 94 (1973).

41   Created by the Public Broadcasting Act 1967; see generally, Franklin, *Mass Media Law*, 3rd edn West, 1986, at 763 ff.

best news and political commentary, remains an underdeveloped institution, lacking the resources to create much original programming on the scale to enjoy the BBC's commanding presence.

Relying instead mainly on its power to regulate commercial broadcasting, the FCC produced rules prescribing coverage of issues of public importance in a fair and balanced way.[42] But these concepts in the American system have lacked the pervasive implications of their British counterparts; they produced something much less than an ethos of public service broadcasting. Thus licensees were not prohibited from offering their own editorial views on public issues.[43] Anyone personally attacked had the right to respond,[44] but impartiality between viewpoints was not a fundamental value of the system.

Nor did opposing viewpoints necessarily require the opportunity of a reply in all cases. Candidates for federal electoral office were entitled to equal time if their opponents were given use of broadcasting facilities,[45] but this principle was less than universal in its effect on political debate. Its narrowness was shown when the Democratic Party failed in its claim to respond to President Eisenhower's broadcasts on the Suez crisis.[46] Congress further eroded the obligation of equality by creating exceptions to allow televised debates between some presidential candidates, without equal opportunity for all.[47] News broadcasts were entirely exempted; as a result of generous wording of this clause, it became possible to show one party convention, but not the other.[48] Fairness, as a principle, thus operated within much narrower confines than in Britain.

American political parties also enjoyed fewer rights of direct access to broadcasting facilities. They were permitted to buy advertising and by law, the same amount of time had to be offered to opponents, if they could afford it.[49] But except to candidates for elected federal office, the broadcasting companies did not have to sell time, if they did not want to. The Democratic Party, in *CBS v DNC*,[50] failed again, this time in its attempt to secure access for the purpose of criticising the Vietnam war, despite its willingness to pay and the frequency of Presidential broadcasts in favour of the war. While many believed that TV coverage helped undermine support for the war, there was in law little to require balanced or evenhanded coverage of the issues.[51] In

---

42   13 FCC 1246, 1249 (1949); upheld in *Red Lion Broadcasting Co. v FCC* 395 US 367 (1969); *CBS v Democratic National Committee* 412 US 94 (1973). See FCC *Fairness Report* (1974), 48 FCC 2d 1.
43   *FCC v League of Women Voters* 468 US 364 (1984).
44   *Red Lion Broadcasting Co. v FCC* 395 US 367 (1967); Franklin, at 820 ff.
45   Section 315, Communications Act, 47 USC; Franklin, at 790 ff.
46   14 RR 720 (FCC 1956).
47   *Johnson v FCC* (1987) US App. DC; Franklin, at 793 ff.
48   Section 315(a), 47 USC.
49   Section 312(a)(7), 47 USC; *CBS v FCC* 453 US 367 (1981).
50   412 US 94 (1973).
51   But see further, Franklin, at 804 ff, where attempts to use the doctrine more expansively are reviewed.

practice, fairness regulation in the US system amounted to little more than the FCC's personal attack rule, and the statutory right of election candidates to equal time.

In *Red Lion*,[52] the Supreme Court chose to uphold the constitutionality of these fairness rules, and to treat broadcasting as different from the press where free speech was in issue. The public interest in vigorous debate, it believed, required regulation of broadcasting to avoid monopolistic private censorship. The court's main focus in this case was thus on the listeners' and viewers' right to diversity of opinion, not on the broadcasters' right to speak unhindered by restrictions.

But later cases have tended to emphasise the broadcasters' right to free speech and to limit the restrictions which may be imposed upon it. In *CBS v DNC*[53] the Supreme Court upheld the broadcasters' right to refuse political advertising as a matter of editorial judgment; in *FCC v League of Women Voters*,[54] it affirmed that broadcasters too had a First Amendment right to offer editorial opinion, even in the case of public broadcasting where funding came mainly from Congress. In *FCC v Listeners Guild*,[55] it upheld the FCC's policy of refusing to regulate programme diversity, thus in effect supporting the broadcasters' editorial freedom to determine programme content. *Red Lion* was not explicitly overruled, but in practice the extent of its departure from a classical free speech model was severely curtailed. In 1987, the FCC drew the obvious conclusion and repealed its own fairness rules.[56]

The FCC argued that repeal would benefit vigorous debate. It believed the fairness rules encouraged broadcasters to eliminate coverage of controversial political issues, rather than face the burden of compliance.[57] Others have identified actual and potential abuse of power for political ends in the operation of FCC regulation, and a tendency for the Commission to favour expressions of conventional opinion over original, innovative viewpoints.[58] Scarcity of channels, the original justification for licensing, is now arguably more of a problem for the newspaper press, where fairness has never been the rule, than it is for broadcasters. In any case, the growth of cable TV since *Red Lion*, has in practice greatly extended the range of broadcasting possibilities and made full First Amendment freedom based on competition a more plausible option.[59]

Yet there is no guarantee that multiplicity of channels alone will ensure diversity of public debate.[60] In reality, cable TV has meant in the US merely

---

52   395 US 367 (1969).
53   412 US 94 (1973).
54   468 US 364 (1984).
55   450 US 502 (1981).
56   *Syracuse Peace Council v Television Station WTVH* 63 Rad. Reg. 2d (P & F) 541, 573 (1987).
57   Fairness Report, (1985) 102 FCC 2d. 143.
58   Powe, *American Broadcasting and the First Amendment,* University of California Press, 1987.
59   *Ibid.*, chapters 11 and 12.
60   Collins, 66 Tex LR 453 (1987); Barron 80 Harv. LR 1641 (1967); Bollinger, 75 Mich. LR 1 (1976).

more entertainment channels, more repeats of old programmes, more narrow special interest programmes, but little in the way of extra public affairs broadcasting except for one cable news network and some tedious 'public access' channels showing 'live' proceedings from Congress or city councils. Something more is needed if advertising and cheap entertainment are not to dominate an expanded British system in the same way.

This diversity of debate the market alone is unlikely to supply; to achieve it will require regulation of some kind, and inevitable control of the range and content of programming. The American experience surely demonstrates that unadulterated free speech in the broadcasting sphere still cannot promise what a free press has traditionally supplied by way of public debate and information. With this in mind it is important to consider the possible implications of change in the regulation of British broadcasting.

Possible Options for Future Regulation

One possibility is simply that all broadcasting adheres to the present BBC/IBA model of public service broadcasting. This would ensure continued diversity and fairness in output, but would not meet demands for greater competition or prove economically attractive if too high a quality of service is demanded for all channels. It is also an approach which the Government has already rejected in the Cable and Broadcasting Act and in more recent proposals for expanded commercial radio and television.[61]

Yet some of these examples show willingness to continue a measure of regulation. They are not evidence of complete conversion to an American-style free speech model of broadcasting. The 1984 Act still requires news programmes to be accurate and impartial,[62] and it requires the Cable Authority to ensure that services do not give undue prominence to religious or political views of particular persons or bodies[63] – in effect an obligation of political balance. Nor are the cable companies themselves allowed to editorialise on such issues.[64] This is a minimal departure only from the existing model. It lessens the obligation to provide the same broad range of services as the BBC and IBA but continues to insist on political fairness.

What this approach does not do however is to require that cable services should offer news or public affairs broadcasting; they are free to choose not to do so,[65] and in that important sense there is a significant retreat from the public service functions of the other broadcasting bodies. Satellite services are

---

61 See Notes 8 and 9 above.
62 Section 10.
63 Section 11(3).
64 Section 11(3).
65 The Cable Authority must take account of the range and diversity of programmes proposed by applicants for licences, however: section 7(2).

specifically freed from any obligation to carry news broadcasts, or to offer a proper balance and wide range in subject matter.[66] Again, while this may not undermine the fairness of any political broadcasting, it will probably ensure that none is offered.

A more radical possibility is to abolish all public service obligations for commercial broadcasting, and leave programme content entirely to market forces. Taken to extremes, such an approach would involve abolition of the IBA and leave the BBC providing the only obligatory public service outlet – if that institution survived abolition of its licence fee and the arrival of a pay-as-you-view system. Whether public affairs programming would still be a significant component of this system would then depend entirely on how the BBC could sell its programmes and on the commercial judgment of the other broadcasting networks. As in America, the likelihood is that advertisers would come to dominate the latter's output and favour blander, uncontroversial matter.

The inescapable conclusion thus appears to be that if public affairs programmes and vigorous, informed debate are valued elements of our broadcasting system, they are best defended by public service regulation on the IBA model and an adequately funded, independent-minded BBC. There is little evidence to suggest that either multiplicity of channels, or a free speech model will by themselves provide any adequate substitute, or justify departure from the present model.

That is not to say that all broadcasting need conform to this ideal. Reduced standards for cable or satellite TV, or local radio, are unobjectionable so long as they do not become the norm. What is needed is a recognition that there is room for diversity in standards of broadcasting to ensure both a continuation of its public service role, and an expanded market, and that this is only likely to be secured by continuing regulation of programme content. In broadcasting, function and form cannot be separated.

---

66   Section 37(2).

Recent Developments in the French Law of the Press in Comparison with Britain

Roger Errera

This essay is an attempt to assess recent developments in the law of the press in France and to compare them to significant elements in the English scene, as seen by a foreign observer.

The Constitutional Protection of Freedom of Expression

Freedom of expression, or, more accurately, of communication is constitutionally protected in French law. The relevant instrument here is Article 11 of the Declaration of the Rights of Man and of the Citizen (1789): 'The free communication of thoughts and of opinions is one of the most precious rights of man; every citizen may therefore speak, write and publish freely, provided he shall be liable for the abuse of this freedom in such cases as are determined by law.' In a series of cases relating to statutes regulating public and private broadcasting or aiming at preventing excessive concentration in the press sector, the Conseil Constitutionnel has strongly affirmed the constitutional status of freedom of communication.[1] Moreover a decision of July 1986 contains a very important dictum: whenever Parliament legislates on fundamental freedoms, it may not suppress a constitutionally guaranteed right.[2]

Roger Errera, Conseilleur d'Etat, was Visiting Professor of French law at University College London in 1983-4, and British Council Senior Research Fellow at the Institute of Advanced Legal Studies in 1987-8. The help of the British Council, of the French Embassy in London, of the Conseil d'Etat and of the Faculty of Laws of University College London is gratefully acknowledged.

1 See the law of the press: Decision No. 84-181 DC, 10-11 October 1984 at 73. RDP 1986, at 395, note Favoreu; AJDA 1984. 684 note Bienvenu; S. Hubac and E. Schoettlk, 'La situation des groupes de presse à la suite de la décision des 10 et 11 Octobre du Conseil constitutionnel et de la promulgation de la loi du 23 octobre 1984', RSC 1985, at 3; L. Favoreu et L. Philip, Les grandes décisions du Conseil Constitutionnel, 4th edn, Sirey, Paris 1986 at 40; Decision No. 9 86-210 29 July 1986, at 110; RDP 1986, 395 note Favoreu. On broadcasting see the following decisions: 81-129 DC, 30-31 October 1981, at 35; RDP 1983 333, note Favoreu; 82-141 DC, 27 July 1982, at 45; 86-217 DC, 18 September 1986, at 141; 88-248, 17 January 1989, JO 18 January 1989, at 754.

2 For a recent and exhaustive analysis of the case-law of the Conseil constitutionnel, see B. Genevois, La jurisprudence du Conseil constitutionnel. Principes directeurs, Editions STH, Paris 1988.

The contrast with the English position does not need many comments. Although the debate on the adoption of a Bill of Rights has been thorough,[3] neither of the two major political parties seems inclined to propose such a reform.

Privacy

'Offensive invasion of privacy is not yet recognised in English law as an independent tort. There is no legal redress available to one whose past life is mercilessly publicized or who is accurately photographed in embarrassing circumstances.'[4] In the past 30 years or so all attempts to create such a right, either through a new statute or by case-law, have failed. The story of private members' bills is a familiar one.[5] The Justice[6] and Younger[7] Reports do not appear to have been very influential in this respect. The Press Council cannot solve the problem and the press will not 'exert itself to ensure that its standards of fair reporting are maintained by all'.[8] In spite of many calls for the introduction of a statutory right of privacy[9] the situation is unchanged. The law of confidentiality has obvious limits in protecting privacy.[10]

---

3   See A. Lester, 'Fundamental Rights in the United Kingdom: the Law and the British Constitution', 125 *University of Pennsylvania Law Review*, 1976 at 337; 'Fundamental Rights: the United Kingdom isolated?', (1984) *Public Law* 46; 'The Constitution: Decline and Renewal' in *The Changing Constitution*, J. Jowell and D. Oliver, eds, Clarendon Press, Oxford, 1985, 273; M. Zander, *A Bill of Rights?*, 3rd edn, Barrie Rose, 1985.

4   de Smith, *Constitutional and Administrative Law*, ed. H. Street and R. Brazier, 5th edn, Pelican Books, 1985, 476 to 477.

5   Lord Mancroft's (1961) and Mr A. Lyon's MP (1967), Mr B. Walden's, (1969), Mr W. Cash's MP, (1987) and Mr J. Browne's (1989). On the first two see R. Wacks, *The Protection of Privacy*, Sweet and Maxwell, London, 1980, at 5 to 9; on Mr Walden's bill see G.D.S. Taylor, 'Privacy and the Public', 34 *MLR* 1971 288. On Mr Browne's see Hansard, House of Commons, 27 January 1989, at 1300 to 1363.

6   Justice, *Privacy and the Law*, 1970.

7   *Report of the Committee on Privacy*, Cmnd 5012, HMSO, 1972.

8   Thus J. Bishop, Chairman of the Association of British Editors, letter to *The Times*, 26 January 1989.

9   See, *inter alia*, M. Bulmer and J. Bell, 'The press and personal privacy. Has it gone too far?', *Political Quarterly* 1985 at 5; and M. Cranston's excellent essays: *The Right to Privacy*, Unserville State Papers, no. 21, n.d.; 'A private space', *Information sur les sciences sociales* – *Social Sciences informations* 14, 1988 and his article 'Make privacy the priority', *The Times*, 26 January 1989; 'Indecent Assault', *The Economist*, 28 January 1989, 'Privacy and the Right to Know', *New Law Journal*, 22 May 1987 at 463. In 1989, in response to a private member's bill on Privacy, the Home Office set up a Committee on 'Privacy and Related Matters' under the chairmanship of David Calcutt Q.C.

10   See, for example, *Stephens v Amery and Others*, Chancery Division, 26 February 1988, *The Independent* Law Report, 27 February 1988; the *Bowley* case: M. Berlins, 'Anne Diamond and the homosexual QC', *Law Magazine* 5 February 1988 at 15 and D. Pannick, 'Personal secrets protected by established legal principles', *The Independent* , 29 January 1988. See also the Law Commission's Working Paper 58, *Breach of Confidence*, 1974 and Report, *Breach of Confidence*, HMSO, 1981, Cmnd 8388. For a general study of the case-law see David J. Seipp, 'English Judicial Recognition of a Right to Privacy', *Oxford Journal of Legal Studies*, vol. 3, no. 3 at 325.

What is indeed striking for a foreign observer is first, the extent to which
the very concept of privacy has been attacked and criticised[11] and is still not
accepted as the basis of a tort; secondly, the fact that the courts have not taken
the initiative of affirming such a right; and thirdly, the contrast between the
almost unanimous discontent with the press invasion of privacy and the
'classic' objections to the creation of a general right to privacy: that it is a
concept so vague as to be almost 'unworkable'; the existence of competing
interests; and the risk of leaving too much discretion to the courts, allied to
the fact that their very 'ability . . . to construe general concepts' is sometimes
doubted or feared.[12]

The way in which, in French law, a right to privacy has been affirmed offers
a sharp contrast with the situation in English law:[13] the right to privacy has
been first a creation of the case-law of the civil courts, no doubt influenced by
academic writings on 'rights of personality' (*les droits de la personnalité*). The
contribution of the courts has been a threefold one. First, they have not given
a general and permanent definition of what is privacy and what is not. They
have, instead, arrived at it gradually (for example, it includes personal and
family life; health; religious belief, etc.). Secondly, this domain is distinct from
that covered by libel law.[14] Privacy also differs from another right, the right
to one's name and image. The legal régime of protection has been defined.
Thirdly, while in libel law (both a criminal and civil matter in French law) the
court must establish a wrongful intent, fault and damage, any interference
with privacy brings a right to reparation. Good faith on the part of the
defendant, truth or the public interest are not defences.

---

11   See G. Marshall, 'The Right to Privacy: A Sceptical View', 21 *McGill Law Journal* 1975
at 242. The article ends with the following sentence 'To be meaningful and effective,
reference to a general right of privacy must be avoided: specific rights of privacy must be
enumerated and defined'. At 254; R. Wacks, 'The Poverty of Privacy', 96 *Law Quarterly
Review* 73 (1980).
12   Hansard, Note 5 above, at 1346.
13   See P. Kayser, *La protection de la vie privée*, 2 vols, Paris, Economics, 1984-5; R.
Badinter, 'Le droit au respect de la vie privée', *JCP* 1968 1. 2136; M. Contamine-Raynaud,
'Le secret de la vie privée' in *L'information en droit privé*, Y. Loussouarn ed., LGDJ, Paris,
1978, at 541; Travaux de l'Association H. Capitant, 13, *La protection de la personnalité*,
Dalloz, 1963 (see in particular J. Nerson, 'La protection de la personnalité en droit privé
francais', at 60); J. Kayser, 'Le secret de la vie privée et la jurisprudence civile' in *Mélanges
Savatier*, Dalloz, Paris, 1961 at 405. For an English comment on the French law of privacy
see R. Redmon-Cooper, 'The Press and the Law of Privacy', *ICLQ* 1985 at 769; for a
comparative analysis see B.S. Markesinis, 'The right to be let alone v. freedom of speech',
Public Law 1986 at 67.
14   Every individual has an exclusive right to his image and its uses and is entitled to
prohibit its dissemination or publication without his special and express consent. See
E. Gaillard, 'La double nature du droit à l'image et ses conséquences en droit positif francais,
D 1984 at 161; J. Ravanas *La Protection des personnes contre la réalisation et la publication
de leur image*, LGDJ, Paris, 1978; D. Acquarone, 'L'ambiguité du droit à l'image', *D* 1985
at 129. On the unlawful uses of photographs for commercial or advertisement purposes see
C.A. Paris, 9 May 1985, *Agence Vandystadt c. Fédération francaise de karaté et autres*,
D 1986 IR 49, note Lindon; *id.* 6 June 1985, *Société Fotogram c. Michel et autres, ibid.*,
TGI Paris, 18 November 1987, *Narbonne c. Société Carter et autres*, *D* 1988. IR 200, note
Lindon.

Parliament came in later on: the statute of 17 July 1970 merely codifies and clarifies the existing case-law and extends the protection, in civil and criminal law, in private life, especially of its 'core' (*l'intimité de la vie privée*).[15] Although the case-law of the Conseil Constitutionnel is not, so far, conclusive on this matter,[16] it is certainly arguable that the right to privacy has now acquired constitutional status and is protected as such, being one of the 'fundamental principles recognised by the laws of the Republic'.[17]

Some areas are still partly unexplored. Here are two interesting examples, from a legal as well as from a cultural point of view. Is information about an individual's money or assets affected by his right to privacy? While some courts have adopted an affirmative answer,[18] recent decisions are more balanced, using the notions of public interest and of whether the information was obtained legitimately and in good faith to determine whether such information is protected by a right to privacy.[19]

Is there a right to be forgotten (*un droit à l'oubli*), the infringement of which could be construed as an invasion of privacy? Two American cases decided half a century ago, *Melvin* and *Sidis*,[20] are sometimes quoted in this respect. The issue they raise is still valid: can the memory of past public events (e.g. a crime, a trial) be revived when it clearly invades privacy? Can the lapse of time have legal effects? Certain recent decisions mention such a right, although not without qualifications.[21]

The powers granted to the civil courts both by Article 9 of the Civil Code and by Article 809, paragraph 1 of the New Civil Procedure Code are sweeping. Under the former the courts may, in addition to the award of damages, order any measures (for example, a seizure, etc.) in order to *prevent* or stop an intrusion into the intimacy of privacy (*l'intimité de la vie privée*). Such injunctions may, in urgent cases, be delivered in interlocutory proceedings. Under Article 809, paragraph 1, of the NCPC the President of the Civil Court is empowered to order, in interlocutory proceedings, any measures that are necessary to prevent imminent harm or put a stop to a manifestly unlawful

---

15   On this statute see J. Pradel, 'Les dispositions de la loi No. 70-463 sur la protection de la vie privée', *D* 1971 14; R. Lindon, 'Les dispositions de la loi du 17 Juillet 1970 relatives à la protection de la vie privée, *JCP* 1970 I. 2357. See Article 9 of the Civil Code.
16   See B. Genevois, *La jurisprudence du Conseil constitutionnel*, Note 2 above at 214.
17   Preamble to the 1946 Constitution, incorporated into the 1958 one.
18   TGI Marseille, 29 September 1982, *Pucciarelli v Rignetti D* 1984 64, note Lindon.
19   CA Paris, 15 January 1987 *D* 1987 2331, note Lindon; CA Paris, 20 October 1987, *Kampf et autre c. Société le Nouvel Observateur du Monde*, *D* 1988 IR 197; CA Paris, 13 January 1988 (2 cases).
20   *Sidis v F.R. Publishing Co.* 113 F.2d., 806 (2d Cir. 1940), cert. denied, 311 US 711 (1940); *Melvin v Reid*, 112 App; 285 (Dist. Ct. App. 1931).
21   See, for example, TGI Paris, 25 March 1987, *L. v S.A. Kenner Parker France et autres*, *D* 1988 199, note Lindon; TGI Paris, 20 April 1983; *JCP* 1983. II 20434, note Lindon; TGI Paris, 4 October 1965, *Segret v Société Rome Paris Films et autres*, *JCP* 1966. II.14482, note G. Lyon-Caen. For a recent example see 'Les exigences de la vertu', *Le Monde*, July 15-16 1984.

trouble (*un trouble manifestement illicite*).[22] This clause has been used in a number of cases between private parties.[23]

The consistent and principled approach of the French courts to the issue of privacy and the fact that Parliament has followed their lead have produced a substantial protection of what is undoubtedly a fundamental right, as well as a welcome measure of legal certainty. The notion of *droits de la personnalité* is here central. Developed first by academic authors and commentators, its aim is to protect the individual's integrity against external interference. As we approach the centennial of this famous essay, it might be worthwhile to recall here that in the 1890 article in the *Harvard Law Review* Warren and Brandeis mentioned the right to the protection of privacy 'as a part of the more general right to the immunity of the person – the right to one's personality'.

Secrecy and Access to Public Documents

Although access to Government documents is not, strictly speaking, a part of freedom of expression, it must, however, be briefly mentioned here.[24] While in France a right of access to Government documents was recognised by statute in 1978,[25] there is no counterpart in English law so far.[26]

Since the publication of the Franks Committee Report in 1972,[27] the extent and uses of official secrecy and of the Official Secrets Act 1911, have been

---

22 On the *référé* procedure see R. Perrot, *Institutions judiciaires*, 3rd edn, Paris Montchestion, 1989; See also P. Kayser, 'Les pouvoirs du juge des référés civil à l'égard de la liberté de communication et d'expression' *D.* 1989, at 11.

23 See TFI Paris, 30 November 1983, *Consorts Hartevelt v Société des Editions modernes*, *D.* 1984. III, note R.L; *Gaz. Pal.* 1984.I.7, note Bertin (Injunction, following an action brought by the family, against a magazine which had published a photograph of the corpse, cut into pieces, of a woman killed by a madman); TGI Paris, 23 May 1987, *Gaz. Pal.* 1987. I. 369 (Temporary injunction, at the opening of the Barbie trial, against a 'revisionist' journal denying the Nazi genocide of the Jews); CA Dijon, 12 January 1988, *Bianco v Balilly et autres*, *D.* 1988. I.R. 134; TGI Versailles, 28 January 1988, *Le Pen c. Unadis*, *Gaz. Pal.* 1988.I.129, note Bertin (Mr Le Pen had declared, in a TV interview, that the mass gassing of the Jews by the Nazis was a 'point of detail'; the court held the statement to be a 'manifestly unlawful trouble' for survivors and their families and ordered part of the judgment to be mentioned on TV). From these and many other cases it is now clear that Article 809 NCPC is used by the courts to protect, beyond privacy, other rights and feelings. See *infra*, at 80 to 81 and P. Kayser, 'Les pouvoirs du juge des référés civils à l'égard de la liberté de communication et d'expression', *D.* 1989 at 11.

24 For a general study see *Public Access to Government-Held Information*, N. Marsh ed, Stevens, London, 1987.

25 See R. Errera, 'The Right of Access to Government Documents. The Reform of the Law in France', (1979) IV, *Human Rights Review*, 23; 'Access to Administrative Documents in France: Reflexions on a Reform', in *Public Access* op. cit. at 87; D. Clark, 'Open Government. The French Experience', *Political Quarterly*, 1986, at 278. For a collection of statutes and regulations relating to administrative acts (access to documents; duty to give reasons) see *Actes administratife. Accès aux documents. Motivation des actes*. Journal officiel. Brochure no. 1470 3rd edn, 1988.

26 N. Marsh, 'Public Access to Government-Held Information in the UK: Attempts at Reform', in *Public Access* op. cit., Note 24 above, at 248.

27 *Departmental Committee on Section 2 of the Official Secrets Act 1911*, Cmnd 5104, 4 vols, HMSO, 1972. On the history of the Act before 1939 see R.M. Thomas, 'The British Official Secrets Act, 1911-1939', *Criminal Law Review*, 1986, at 491.

among the most debated issues in Britain.[28] The Act is reformed by the Official Secrets Act 1989.[29] A complete discussion of this issue would be beyond the scope of this essay.

What would have happened if the *Spycatcher* affair had taken place in France? According to civil service law, all civil servants are bound by the rules of professional secrecy.[30] The latter is defined by the Penal Code. Any infringement of professional secrecy is an offence. The penalties incurred are imprisonment or fine. This applies as well to the professions.[31] A breach of secrecy by a civil servant may of course lead to disciplinary action against him. In addition, civil servants are also bound, by law, by another obligation, that of *discretion professionelle*; this applies to 'all facts, informations or documents they may know through their activities'.[32]

The criminal law relating to official secrets is contained in Articles 75 and 78 of the Penal Code. Article 75 makes it an offence that may be punished by heavy jail terms (10 to 12 years) for any person, being in possession through his activities or status of any information or document that must be kept secret in the interest of national defence (or the disclosure of which might lead to the disclosure of a defence secret) and without an intention of treason or of espionage, to reproduce it or cause it to be reproduced, or to disclose it to a third and unauthorised party or to the public. Article 78 relates to a less grave offence; it is directed against anyone who, without intention of treason or of espionage, discloses to a third and non-authorised party or to the public, military information that has not been made public by the competent authorities and the disclosure of which is obviously of such a nature as to cause harm to national defence.

Under press law no other specific remedy would have been available in *Spycatcher*. Under *civil* law, however, Article 809 of the *Nouveau Code de*

---

28   J. Aitken, *Officially Secret*, Weidenfeld and Nicolson, London, 1971; D. Hooper, *Official Secrets. The Use and Abuse of the Act*, Secker and Warburg; J. Jacob, 'Some Reflections on Governmental Secrecy', *Public Law*, 1974, at 25; C. Seymour-Ure, 'G.B.', in *Government Secrecy in Democracies*, I. Galnoor ed., Harper and Row, New York, 1977; J. Michael, 'Official Secrecy in Britain', *Index on Censorship*, January-February 1987; J. Michael, *The Politics of Secrecy*, Penguin 1982.

P. Birkinshaw, *Freedom of Information: The Law, the Practice and the Ideal*, Weidenfeld and Nicolson, London 1988; P. Jenkins, 'Not so free speech in Britain', *New York Review of Books*, 8 December 1988.

29   See *Reform of Section 2 of the Official Secrets Act 1911*, HMSO, 1978, Cmnd 7285; *Open Government*, HMSO 1979, Cmnd 1520; *Reform of Section 2 of the Official Secrets Act 1911*, HMSO, 1988, Cmnd 408.

30   Article 26 paragraph 1 of the Law of 13 July 1983 on the Rights and Duties of Civil Servants.

31   On the scope and limits of secrecy in French law see: Travaux de l'association, H. Capitant 25, *Le Secret et le droit*, Paris, Dalloz, 1974; F. Warenbourg-Auque, 'Reflexions sur le secret professionnel en droit francais', in *ibid.* above; 105 M. Delmas-Marty, 'A propos du secret professionnel', D 1982 267; B. Decheix, 'Un droit de l'homme mis à mal: le secret professionnel' D 1983 133.

32   Paragraph 2 of Article 26 of the law of 13 July 1983, quoted above at Note 30.

Procédure Civile could arguably have been used,[33] although there does not seem to be any precedent in which the Government has obtained from the courts an injunction enjoining the press or a publisher from publishing an article or information.

How is the law enforced? In the absence of available statistics, it is impossible to know whether alleged breaches of secrecy, within the meaning of Article 378 of the Penal Code, often lead to disciplinary action against civil servants. Criminal prosecution against them on the basis of Article 378, or 75 or 78 of the Penal Code is extremely rare.

Had *Spycatcher* happened in France, it is extremely unlikely, in my opinion, that the Government would have initiated legal proceedings before a foreign court. The two other remaining courses of action would have been to prosecute the author and to request his extradition from the country of residence. It is not very probable that the Government would have used them. Disciplinary or criminal proceedings against retired civil servants are almost unheard of.

Fair Trial, Free Speech and Open Justice

This is an area in which a balance has to be struck between several rights and between several legitimate and competing interests: freedom of expression, as guaranteed and defined both in domestic and in international law, especially under Article 10 of the European Human Rights Convention; the right to a fair trial; the necessary protection of the independence and integrity of the courts and the principle of open justice. In France as elsewhere this issue has been debated in recent years.[34] It might be useful to attempt a brief comparison of the law and practice in France and in the UK before, during and after a trial.

It is clear that French law contains here a great, even excessive number of clauses prohibiting the publication of information relating to the course of justice. Although the justification of most of them is evident (the protection of minors, of the administration of justice, or of privacy) this is not the case for others. These provisions have been inserted into the law in a haphazard way, due to circumstances that may have disappeared since, and without any general conception. An overall review followed by some reform has been

---

33   The president of the civil court is empowered to order, in interlocutory proceedings, any measures that are necessary to prevent imminent harm or put a stop to a manifestly unlawful trouble (*trouble manifestment illicite*).

34   See *Rapport de la Commission presse-justice*, Paris 1985 (The committee was chaired by the author); *Justice pénale, police et presse*, preface by R. Errera, Cujas, Paris, 1988.

overdue. While some of these prohibitions are respected by the press and enforced, the case of others is somewhat different.[35]

The legal limitations on what may be published before trial are not many. They relate to the protection of minors,[36] of the administration of justice,[37] of privacy[38] or of national defence.[39] There is no equivalent in French law of the English law of contempt. This is the main difference between the two countries.[40]

Restrictions on reporting during a trial are few. In all *civil* cases, courts are empowered to prohibit the reporting of the case.[41] Such a power seems not to be used at all. The reporting of certain trials is prohibited by law: family cases (divorce, paternity, separation); when the proceedings are held in camera; and abortion trials. The same rule applies to juvenile delinquent cases[42] and to treason and espionage.[43] While prohibitions relating to family and juvenile cases are strictly enforced – and rightly so – all others have become totally obsolete. (A good example is the rule that prohibits the reporting of libel cases when the allegations relate to facts older than 10 years or to private life.)[44]

Under French law it is an offence to criticise and discredit (*jeter le discrédit*) a judicial decision in such a manner as to harm the authority of justice or the independence of the judges.[45] There is some case-law about this clause which makes strange reading. The Committee of Inquiry on the Press and the Judiciary recommended its repeal in 1985.[46]

---

35   For a detailed study of the law and proposed reforms, see *Rapport* quoted above Note 34 at 64 ff.

36   It is forbidden to publish any document or illustration relating to the identity of delinquent juveniles (Article 14, paragraph 4, of the *Ordonnance* of 2 February 1945, on Youth) or to minors who have left their family or institution (Article 39 bis of the Law of 29 July 1881 on the Press). The latter prohibition may, however, be waived upon a request from the family, the administration or a court.

37   It is forbidden to publish any criminal procedure, acts or documents before they are read in open court (Article 38 of the Law of 29 July 1881). It is an offence to publish, before the decision of a court, commentaries the aim of which is to constitute pressure relating to the declaration of witnesses or to the decision of the court (Article 227 of the Penal Code).

38   In rape cases it is forbidden to publish the name of the victim, unless she consents to it in writing (Article 39 quinquiés of the Law of 29 July 1881).

39   An extreme case is Article 79-6 of the Penal Code which prohibits the publication of any information relating to steps taken to arrest and prosecute authors of crimes of treason and espionage. For an analysis of that clause and a suggestion to amend or repeal it, see *Rapport* quoted above, Note 34, at 84.

40   A. Arlidge and D. Eady, *The Law of Contempt*, Sweet & Maxwell, London, 1982; C.J. Miller, *Contempt of Court*, 2nd edn, Oxford University Press, 1988; S. Bailey, 'The Contempt of Court Act 1981', *Modern Law Review* 1982, at 301.

41   Article 39 of the Law of July 1881 on the Press.

42   Ordonnance of 2 February 1945, quoted above, N. 36.

43   Article 79-6 of the Penal Code, quoted above, N. 39.

44   See N. 41 above.

45   Article 226 of the Penal Code. On this clause see D. Mayer, 'L'Article 226 du code pénal et la liberté d'expression', *JCP* 1975 I 2738 and Rapport quoted above, N. 35, at 49 to 55.

46   Rapport, at 55.

How can we compare this situation with English law and practice?[47] It is clear that the law gives English courts wider powers in relation to the press and that, as a consequence, the freedom of the latter is somewhat restricted. The absence of the general notion of contempt in French law[48] is central to any parallel between the two countries;[49] the fact that no French press case has yet been referred to the Human Rights Commission in Strasbourg is another relevant difference; no *Sunday Times* or *Harman* cases here.[50] And finally, the absence of the reporting restrictions contained in section 4(2) (postponing of a report of the proceedings[51] and prohibition of the publication of a name or of another matter) of the Contempt of Court Act 1981 is also a notable difference.

My feeling is that French law does not protect as it should either the rights of the individual in relation to the press or the right to a fair trial when there is 'a substantial risk of prejudice to the administration of justice', to quote section 4(2) of the 1981 Act. The consequences are well-known and have been frequently criticised.[52] No Government has yet proposed to change the law. It could do so in one of three ways: create a new tort; create a new offence; introduce into French law the notion of contempt. The two last courses seem excluded. The first one was proposed by the Report of the Committee of Inquiry on the Press and the Judiciary in 1985 but has not yet been adopted.[53]

A Special Protection for the Press?

The question of the protection to be afforded to the press and to journalists has been a matter of debate in the United States as well as in Britain and France for the past 15 years. The theoretical issues are considered in Andrew Lewis's essay in this collection. The discussion has concentrated on two main points: may journalists whose testimony is requested by a court (or grand jury in the United States, or a *juge d'instruction* in France) refuse to testify or to disclose

---

47 On the law of the press in Britain see M. Supperstone, 'Press Law in the United Kingdom', in *Press Law in Modern Democracies. A Comparative Study*, P. Lahav, ed., Longman, New York and London, 1981 at 9 ff; E. Barendt, *Freedom of Speech*, Clarendon Press, Oxford 1985; G. Robertson and A.G.L. Nicol, *Media Law, The Rights of Journalists and Broadcasters*, Oyez Longman, London, 1984.

48 Article 12 of the Nouveau Code de Procédure Civile has a different scope and applies only to parties in civil proceedings.

49 On section 2(2) of the Contempt of Court Act, 181 see *Attorney-General v English* [1983] AC 116; M. Redmont 'Of black sheep and too much wool', *Cambridge Law Journal* 1983 at 9. On contempt at common law see *Attorney-General v News Group Newspapers Ltd*, 19 February 1988, Law Report, *The Independent*, 20 February 1988.

50 For a French comment on these cases see P. Kinder, 'Sur la liberté de la presse en Grande-Bretagne: de l'affaire *Sunday Times* à l'affaire *Harriet Harman* ou les tribulations du contempt of court', *RDP* 1983, at 285.

51 See *R v Horsham Justices ex parte Farquharson* [1982] QB 762, 269; *R v Arundel Justices ex parte Westminster Press Ltd* [1985] 1 WLR 708.

52 See R. Errera, preface to *Justice pénale, police et presse*, quoted above, Note 35.

53 See *Rapport* at 15 ff.

their sources of information? Should searches and seizures be allowed on newspapers' or broadcasters' premises?

Several arguments may be adduced in favour of such a protection, that is, of a right for a journalist to refuse to answer questions related to his sources of information. The first is freedom of the press and of information. For a journalist to reveal his sources of information or even to know that he will have to disclose them would hinder the gathering of information and have what the Americans like to call a 'chilling effect'. A second argument comes from professional ethics and custom: a journalist is not supposed to disclose his sources.

Against the granting of such a protection, which is in fact a privilege, there is no lack of arguments either: privileges and immunities should be granted with extreme caution and only when a pressing public interest or social need justifies them. In addition, to collaborate with the courts, when such collaboration is lawfully requested, is both an individual's duty under the law of the country, and an action that promotes a public interest; granting a privilege to journalists may endanger the rights of all to the good and fair administration of justice. Such a privilege may also be the source of abuses, or might well, in the future, have adverse effects on the press itself.

Another argument, of a different nature, is that such an immunity would not, in practice, be of real help to the press, in the same way as the absence of it has not affected, so far, the process of news-gathering. Those who speak to newsmen and provide information to the press do it for a variety of motives and will anyhow continue to do so. Besides, assuming we accept the principle of such a protection, its scope is not easy to state exactly; will it cover only 'confidential' information received by journalists *qua* journalists? Will it apply to all that has been learnt by them during the exercise of their trade? If so, when is a journalist *not* on duty? Would exceptions to such a privilege be allowed? If so, which ones? The interest of justice? The prevention of crime? The defence of the journalist himself? The solution of American case-law seems to be that journalists cannot claim a First Amendment right to refuse to disclose their sources when called as witnesses before a grand jury or a court.[54] This has generated an interesting debate.[55] The scope of the protection afforded by the state 'shield laws' is uncertain.[56]

---

54   *New York Times Cy v Jascalevich*, 439 US 1301 (1978); *In re Farber*, 78 NJ 259; 394 A2d. 330; cert. denied, 439 US 997 (1978).

55   See *Newsmen's Privilege. Hearings before the subcommittee on constitutional rights of the Committee on the Judiciary*, US Senate, 93rd Congress, 20,21,22,27 February; 13,14 March 1973 GPO Washington, 1973; P. Stewart, 'Or of the press' 26 *Hastings Law Journal* (1975); A. Lewis, 'A preferred position for journalists?', 7 *Hofstra Law Review*, at 595 (1979); R. Dworkin, 'The Farber Case. Reporters and Informers', in *A Matter of Principle*, Harvard University Press, Cambridge 1985, at 373; 'Is the Press losing the First Amendment?' *ibid.*, at 381 A. Soifer, 'Freedom of the Press in the United States', in *Press Law in Modern Democracies*, quoted above, n. 47, at 112.

56   See Soifer, above, at 132, n.212.

Under French law professional secrecy as stated by Article 378 of the Penal Code makes it the duty of the members of certain professions not to disclose any information connected with the exercise of it. It does *not* apply to journalists.[57] The current procedural law (criminal or civil) contains no privilege or immunity whatsoever for journalists. The Report of the Committee of Inquiry on the Press and the Judiciary (1985) did not propose any changes to the legislation. If and when a journalist, called as a witness, refuses to testify before a court or refuses to disclose his sources of information, it is for the court to decide whether this is an offence (punishable usually by a fine) or whether, in view of all the circumstances, the journalist may invoke a 'legitimate motive' and thus be excused.[58] Such *causes célèbres* as the *Branzburg* and the *Farber* cases in the USA have not so far occurred in France.[59] The tendency of these courts is not to press on newsmen questions concerning their sources and, in general, not to convict them if they keep silent.

In Britain section 10 of the Contempt of Court Act 1981 affords some protection to journalists.[60] It is interesting to compare the case-law[61] before and after[62] the reform of 1981. The wording of section 10 of the Contempt of Court Act and the circumstances of the *Guardian* and *Warner* cases have led to decisions that do not seem to afford much protection to the press.

Searches and seizures carried out on the premises of newspapers or broadcasting stations are bound to provoke reactions. This is what has happened in the United States, in Britain and in France, the result being a degree of legislative protection in two of these countries. In the United States the change came about rather quickly. Commenting on the *Stanford Daily* decision[63] the *Economist* wrote: 'Unfortunately the press as an institution

---

57 See Rapport at 143 ff.

58 *Ibid.*, at 147; for a recent example of an imposition of a fine see *Le Monde*, 13 May 1988.

59 See on the subject: L. Hugueney, 'Rapport sur le secret professionnel "des journalistes"', *Revue pénitentiaire*, 1924, at 2; E. Derieux, 'Le secret professionnel du journaliste', *La Croix*, 16 December 1982; 'Le secret professionnel du journaliste', *Trimedia*, Summer 1979, at 18; G. Memeteau, 'La question du secret professionnel du journaliste'; *Gaz.Pal.* February 13,14 at 9.

60 'No court may require a person to disclose, nor is any person guilty of contempt of court for refusing to disclose the source of information contained in a publication for which he is responsible unless it be established to the satisfaction of the court that disclosure is necessary in the interests of justice or national security or for the prevention of disorder or of crime.'

61 *Attorney-General v Mulholland* (1963) 1 QB 477; *British Steel Corporation v Granada TV Ltd* (1981) AC 1096; *Attorney-General v Lundin* (1982) 75 Cr App R 90. See Y. Cripps, 'Judicial Proceedings and refusals to disclose the identity of sources of information', *Cambridge Law Journal* 43 1984, at 266.

62 *Secretary of State for Defence v Guardian Newspapers* [1985] AC 339 HL. See R. Pyper, 'Sarah Tisdall, Ian Wilmore and the Civil Servant's Right to Leak', *Political Quarterly*, 1985, at 72; *In re an inquiry under the Company Securities (Insider Dealing) Act 1985*, House of Lords, 10 December 1987: Law Report, *The Independent*, 11 December 1987; *In re an inquiry under the Company Securities (Insider Dealing) Act 1985*, Chancery Division, 26 January 1988; Law Report, *The Independent*, 27 January 1988.

63 *Zurcher v Stanford Daily* 436 YS 547 (1978).

(if it can be called that) has not lately enjoyed any great popularity with the American public as a whole, and so it is not much use expecting in this case the kind of strong popular pressure that is usually required to get Congress to take some spontaneous action.'[64] Wherever the pressure came from, the Privacy Act 1980 was passed,[65] prohibiting searches and seizures in newspapers' premises when the offence has been committed by a third party, unless the pressing and unavoidable necessity of the operation is clearly established.

After much debate, including a sharp division of opinion within the press itself, legislation containing a protection for the press was enacted in Britain in 1984. It is now contained in section 13 of the Police and Criminal Evidence Act 1984.[66] But other laws (e.g. section 2 of the Official Secrets Act 1911) allow searches based on a warrant.[67] Another issue is related to the right of the police to obtain from the press films or unused negatives taken by cameramen of riot scenes.[68]

In France a number of searches and seizures in newspapers or broadcasting stations have been ordered either by a *juge d'instruction* or by the state prosecutor (*Parquet*).[69] This is entirely lawful. These have provoked hostile reactions from the press, the main arguments being the fear of 'fishing expeditions' and the refusal to become 'auxiliaries' of the police. Commenting on these issues the Report of the Committee of Inquiry on the Press and the Judiciary recommended that the *juge d'instruction* or the prosecutor should be present during these searches, that the exact aim of such searches should be stated with reasonable clarity and precision in order to avoid 'fishing expeditions', or the temptation of them, and that such operations should not in any way constitute an obstacle to the free exercise of the journalists' or of the press's activities, nor the source of undue delay to the publication or

---

64   *The Economist* 10 June 1978, 'Sleuths in the newsroom'.

65   42 USC paragraph 2000a, 94 stat. 1879 (1980). For a criticism of such protection, see A. Lewis, *loc. cit.* and 'Press Bill strikes a Blow for Liberty', *The New York Times*, 12 December 1978.

66   See M. Zander, *The Police and Criminal Evidence Act 1984*, Sweet & Maxwell, London 1985 at 22.

67   For example, the searches conducted in the *Zircon* case at the Glasgow offices of the BBC and at the *New Statesman* (1987). For details see P. Thornton, *Decade of Decline: Civil Liberties in the Thatcher Years*, 1989, chapter 2.

68   See *Re an application under section 9 of the Police and Criminal Evidence Act 1984* 26 May 1988, Law Report, *The Independent*, 27 May 1988.

69   In Lille, acting upon instructions (*commission rogatoire*) from the *juge d'instruction* the police seized unused negatives at a local television station and some photographs at the local Agence France Presse office. This followed a demonstration during which someone had been injured. In the same year another *juge d'instruction* in Paris requested and obtained from a state television channel the recording of a programme showing a father who had unlawfully kept his child with him against a court order. The same happened twice at the Paris offices of *Paris Match* in theft cases. For a typical reaction of journalist's unions see the statement published in *Le Monde*, 22–23 January 1984.

broadcasting of material (unless, of course, a *court* orders a seizure). If need be, photocopies of the relevant documents or material should be made available.[70]

Limits to Freedom of Expression: Three Recent Debates

Three recent debates relating to two books and to movies have been the occasion to ask the question again: what are the proper limits to freedom of expression? The results, in the courts and in Parliament, provide some food for thought.

The first example relates to incitement to suicide. In 1982 a book, *Suicide, Mode d'emploi (Suicide, How to do it)* was published in France. It contained a detailed and precise account of the various means that could be used to commit suicide. The book was debated and much criticised. Although suicide is not an offence in French law, the very existence and availability of such a book raised moral as well as legal issues.[71] Was there anything in the law, it was asked, against the book? The matter was first discussed in Parliament, then in the courts. There was nothing in the Law of the Press of 29 July 1881.[72] Civil law was tried: a young man had committed suicide. The book was found near his bed. The parents sued the author and the publishers for damages, alleging that the book had contributed to the suicide. The court rejected their claim, in the absence of any causal link between the book and the act.[73]

After civil law, criminal law; under Article 63, paragraph 2, of the French Penal Code it is an offence to abstain voluntarily from helping someone who is in danger whenever such an action does not create a risk for oneself or for third parties. A Mr B. wrote to one of the authors of the book, asking for information on the methods described in it, and what was the lethal dose of a medicine he was taking (he suffered from depression). The author obliged and answered twice, first recommending an excess of medicine as the 'best' method, then indicating the number of pills to be taken. B. then committed suicide. The parents initiated criminal proceedings against the author. The lower court and the appeals court convicted and sentenced him under Article 63-2 (six months in jail, suspended, a fine, plus damages). The Cour de Cassation upheld the conviction, on the grounds that it was clear that B.'s

---

70 Rapport at 147.
71 INSERM *Etudes epidemiologiques, Suicides et tentatives de suicide aujourd'hui.* On suicide see J. Baechler, *Les suicides*, preface by R. Aron, Calmann-Lévy, Paris, 1975.
72 French law punishes incitement to or apologia for a number of crimes.
73 See TGI Paris, 23 January 1985. *D* 1985. 418, note Calais; see also, for a case involving a pamphlet published by an association promoting the right to die with dignity, TGI Paris, 25 January 1984, *D* 1984 486, note Mayer.

situation necessitated prompt intervention, that the author was thus bound in law to help him, and that he did nothing of the sort – quite the reverse.[74]

The debate then took on another dimension: should the law remain what it was, that is, of not much help to the public or to the families of victims (the case described above seems to have been a rather exceptional one) or should a new clause be introduced in the Penal Code against such writings? The latter course was chosen. A Private Member's Bill had been introduced in Parliament in 1983. It went too far.[75] In 1986 the Government introduced its own bill, which became the law of 31 December 1987 (Articles 318-1 and 318-2 of the Penal Code).[76] Its contents can be summed up as follows: it is an offence to assist a suicide that has been attempted or committed. The penalty is higher when the victim is under 15. It is also an offence to publish propaganda or advertisements by whatever means in favour of products or methods indicated (*préconisées*) as means to commit suicide.

What would have been the reaction in Britain had such a book been published here and such actions brought before the courts? I do not know. I have found nothing on the matter in the 'law and morality' debate.[77] The issues raised are many and go beyond the question of freedom of expression: should incitement to an act which most people in society clearly see as bad or wrong, but which is definitely *not* an offence, be punishable under criminal law? A parallel could be drawn here with prostitution – *mutadis mutandis*. If so, should we resist the temptation or the urge, prompted by moral outrage, to legislate in an age where the trend seems to be towards decriminalisation in matter of mores and private conduct?[78] But can suicide be considered as a purely private act?

The second example related to cases of movies which were perceived as an outrage to their belief by a number of Roman Catholic organisations because

---

74   TGI Paris, 20 November 1985, *D* 1986 369; CA Paris, 28 November 1986; Cass Crim, 26 April 1988; see text and comment in J. Borricand, 'La répression de la provocation au suicide: de la jurisprudence à la loi', *JCP* 1988 I. 3359.

75   Proposition de loi no. 337, annexe au procès verbal de la séance du 24 Mai 1983, Sénat. The Bill made it an offence to incite to suicide, to help commit it wherever there had been an attempted suicide or a suicide and to make propaganda for suicide.

76   On the law of 31 December 1987 see M. Gendrel, 'Commentaire de la loi no. 87-1133 du 31 Decembre 1987 tendant à reprimer la provocation au suicide', *D* 1988 171; J. Borricand, *loc. cit.*; J. Pralus-Dupuy, 'La répression de la provocation au suicide, commentaire de la loi', *RDSS* 1988 203; F. Zenati, note RTDC 1988 427.

77   H.L.A. Hart, *Law, Liberty and Morality*, OUP 1963; P. Devlin, *The Enforcement of Morals*, OUP 1965. See also *Public and Private Morality*, ed. S. Hampshire, Cambridge University Press, 1978; *Morality and the Law*, ed. Richard A. Wasserstrom, Wadsworth, Belmont (California), 1971; *Law, Morality and Society. Essays in honour of H.L.A. Hart*, ed. P.M.S. Hacker and J. Raz, Clarendon Press, Oxford 1977.

78   The issue has been raised by Guizot as early as 1821. See his *Des conspirations et de la justice politique*, Paris 1821, in *Des conspirations et de la justice politique. De la peine de mort en matière politique*, Paris, Fayard, 1984 at 17.

A number of European countries have in their criminal legislation clauses directed against such publications. See *Rapport de M. Dailly au nom de la commission des lois*, Sénat, No. 359, annexe au procès-verbal de la séance du 24 Mai 1983.

of the title or because of the contents of the advertisement or of the movie itself. The courts were asked in interlocutory proceedings under Article 809 NCPC, to suppress the posters, or ban the film or ban certain scenes. In one case the court ordered posters to be removed.[79] In another case, the courts refused to issue an injunction, in the absence of 'manifestly unlawful trouble' and on the ground of freedom of expression.[80] In the case relating to Scorsese's film, *The Last Temptation of Christ*, the court ordered that an announcement be added to all advertisements for the film stating that the film originated from Kazantzakis's novel and was not an adaptation of the Gospels.[81] Any parallel with Britain should take into account that blasphemy is not an offence under French law, unlike English law[82] and that there is, under French law, separation between the church and the state.

The third example relates to Salman Rushdie's book, *The Satanic Verses*. In June and July 1989 the Paris civil court delivered no fewer than four judgments on it. First a number of individuals and Muslim associations asked the court to ban the book and order its seizure. They also asked the court to order the publisher to provide the court with a copy so that the court could appoint an expert to report on its 'blasphemous, profane and racist' character.

Two judgments of 6 June 1989, rejected both claims.[83] These being interlocutory proceedings the court had jurisdiction only to prevent imminent damage or to put an end to a 'manifestly unlawful trouble'. This could not be the case here, the court held, since the book had not yet been published and its publication was not imminent. The court also refused to order the publisher to provide a copy: this would amount to ordering him to publish the book at a time not chosen by him and forcing him to show the book before publishing it. This would be unlawful: according to the law a publisher is liable for what he publishes, but only after publication.

A third action was then brought. The same plaintiffs asked the court to order the seizure and banning of the book, on the grounds that it violated French group libel law and that it incited to religious hatred and discrimination, which is an offence. They relied on Articles 493 and 812 of

---

79 See TGI Paris, 23 October 1984, and CA Paris, 26 October 1984; *Gaz.Pal.* 1984, at 727. The movie was Godard's *Ave Maria*. The posters showed a half-naked woman on the cross, a scene that did not exist in the film.

80 TGI Paris, 28 January 1985; CA Paris, 13 May 1985; *Gaz.Pal.* 28 May 1985; Cass. Civ. 21 July 1987; *Gaz.Pal.* 30 September to 1 October 187 577; CA Dijon, 22 March 1988 D 1988 IR. 141 *Gaz.Pal.* 29-31 May 1988.

81 TGI Paris, 22 September 1988; CA Paris, 27 September 1988; *Gaz.Pal.* 21-22 October 1988. The latter decision quotes Article 10 of the European Human Rights Convention and Article 10 of the Declaration of the Rights of Man and of the Citizen (1789). For an older case, decided by the Conseil d'Etat, where the banning of a film by the Government was quashed, see Conseil d'Etat, 24 January 1975, *Ministre de l'Information c. Société Rome-Paris-Films*, Rec., p.571; concl. Rougevin-Baville, *RDP* 1975 286.

82 *R v Lemon* and *R v Gay News Ltd* [1978] 3 WLR 404; *Whitehouse v Lemon* (1978) 68 Cr App R 381; *Lemon* (1979) AC 617, see J.R. Spencer, 'Blasphemy: the Law Commission's Working Paper', (1981) *Criminal Law Review*, at 810.

83 See *Le Monde*, 1 and 10 June 1989.

the NCPC which allow a plaintiff to bring an action in which the procedure is *not* contested (that is, it is *ex parte*). This is permitted whenever the case is urgent and when the nature of the order sought demands the absence of adversarial procedure.[84] They failed: the court held that in the circumstances these conditions were not met.[85]

The fourth action resulted in an interesting judgment. It rested on Article 809 of the NCPC relating to interlocutory proceedings. The court rejected the petition, which relied on several grounds. First the plaintiffs claimed that the book was in breach of Article 9 of the Civil Code on the protection of privacy,[86] in that it gravely offended the religious beliefs of Muslims through the profanation of the Prophet Mohamed. The court held that although religious feelings belong to the sphere of privacy the plaintiffs could not establish that the book constituted an intrusion into their private belief or disclosed facts related to it.

The plaintiffs also based their action on several sections of the law of the press of 1881. Under Article 34 of that statute it is an offence to defame the memory of dead persons. However only the heirs have *locus standi* to sue, and only if they also have been libelled. One plaintiff claimed he was a descendant of the Prophet, a bold assertion indeed. This, the court replied, did not mean that he was an heir or that he himself had been libelled by the book.

Under Article 34 it is also an offence to libel a foreign head of state. But only he may bring an action. This claim was therefore also dismissed.

The most serious claim rested on Article 32 of the statute, which makes it an offence to libel any person or group of persons because of their origin or their membership of an ethnic, national, racial or religious group. Inter-locutory proceedings were possible if such an offence (on the substance of which a civil court had no jurisdiction) was self-evident. The court held that this was not the case, for the following reasons. Rushdie's book was a novel, without any historical pretension. It was a work of fiction in which a constant stream of words, images, actions and characters moved along in space and time. As such it could not harm the image of the Prophet. It might be, the court then added, that certain pages of the book could shock a believer and make him feel that his faith was under threat. But, the court said, nobody is bound to read a book.

The decision goes much further: even assuming that the book could have constituted a blow against the respect to which religious beliefs and feelings are entitled, its seizure — an exceptional infringement of freedom of expression — could be warranted only if the blow could be regarded as constituting a 'manifestly unlawful trouble'. This was not the case here.

---

84   See on this procedure Perrot, Note 22 above at 145.
85   TGP Paris, 22 July 1989; see *Le Monde*, 23 July 1989.
86   See *supra*, at 68.

Repeating that freedom of conscience and the right of everyone to respect for his beliefs must be protected against aggressive intrusion or 'illegitimate provocation' the court noted three facts. The book had only been sent to booksellers who had asked for copies. There had been little, if any, advertisement of it. Further, the publisher had undertaken in court to keep to this policy. The court accepted this undertaking.[87] The judgments have not been appealed.

Conclusion

Further observations would be in order, comparing the situation in the United Kingdom and France. A foreign observer cannot but note the number of cases relating to freedom of expression in the UK: *Sunday Times*, *Harman*, the *Crossman Diaries*, the *Guardian/Tisdall* case, *Spycatcher*, etc. He is also bound to note that these were not criminal cases but civil ones in which the issue was whether the court would issue an injunction restraining the press or an author from publishing something. Equivalent actions do not seem to have existed in France. The second remark is a question: could it be that, while there seem to be more restrictions in the UK, the rights of the individual are better protected? A definite answer would demand a thorough comparative study of the law of libel, privacy and contempt.

---

87   TGI Paris, 29 July 1989; see *Le Monde*, 1 August 1989.

Bentham's View of Journalists' Privilege and The Independent Case*

A.D.E. Lewis

My intention in this essay is to provoke thought not just on the narrow issue of the supposed privilege of journalists and its intellectual foundation but on the usefulness of reflecting on this question in the light of Bentham's wider view of the law of evidence.

I am presently preparing a new edition of Bentham's introductory work on the Law of Evidence known from the title it bears in the hitherto standard edition as *An Introductory View to the Rationale of Evidence*, but which is better called *The Introduction to the Rationale of Evidence*. Bentham's major work on evidence is the *Rationale of Judicial Evidence* published in 1827 in five volumes in an edition prepared by John Stuart Mill from Bentham's manuscripts. The *Introductory View* was not published until the Bowring edition of Bentham's Works a decade after Bentham's death. This too was prepared from the original manuscripts in Bentham's hand. These still survive amongst the 190-odd boxes of Bentham's manuscripts preserved at University College London, which form the basis for the current *Collected Works* edition of Bentham. Regrettably the manuscript material utilised by J.S. Mill for his edition of the *Rationale of Judicial Evidence* has disappeared. However, there is reason to believe, not least from the facts that the edition was prepared during Bentham's life and presumably with his co-operation, that this represents a more faithful reproduction of Bentham's original text than can be shown to be the case with the Bowring text of the *Introductory View*. In neither work does Bentham deal expressly with the issue of journalists' privilege, but in the context of his general argument for a free Natural system of procedure and evidence to replace the Common Law's Technical system, he considers the constraints which might properly and

---

A.D.E. Lewis M.A., LL.B, Senior Lecturer in Law at University College London

* This contribution is a largely unamended version of the last seminar paper in the series 'The Freedom of the Press?' given in the Faculty of Laws, University College London in the Spring Term 1988. As such it bears traces of an attempt to stimulate general discussion on the range of issues raised in the course of the series.

legitimately be placed upon his broad requirement that everything should be produced before the court save only where preponderant delay, vexation or expense would ensue.[1]

It seems topical to examine the issue of journalistic privilege raised by *The Independent* case[2] against the background of Bentham's general argument, to see whether one might draw legitimate conclusions from the working out of his theory for the supposed right of journalists to conceal their sources. Broadly put, would Bentham concede to journalists this privilege and if so would he be correct to do so within the terms of his own assumptions? Such an approach may not only lead us to a finer understanding of the issues involved in *The Independent* case, it may also enable us to form a view about the continued relevance of Bentham's views on evidence.

It seems appropriate, at this remove in time, to provide a brief factual resumé of the issues in *The Independent* case. I shall follow this with a sketch of the relevant arguments from the *Introductory View*, and conclude with appropriate applications of Bentham's argument for *The Independent* case.

The Independent Case

Jeremy Warner, a journalist first on *The Times* and then with *The Independent*, published accounts in 1985 and 1986 of the consideration of certain cases by the Monopolies and Merger Commission. His reports subsequently led Inspectors appointed under the provisions of section 177 of the Financial Services Act 1986 to form the impression that he was receiving information from a source whose activities might fall within the purview of their investigation. The Inspectors therefore called Mr Warner before them, whereupon he declined to answer any of their questions 'because if I tell you what I was told that would give you some help presumably in identifying the sort of people I talk to about my stories'. In pursuance of section 178 of the Financial Services Act the matter came before Hoffmann J in the Chancery Division of the High Court. He determined that Warner had a reasonable excuse within

1   J. Bentham, 'An Introductory View of the Rationale of Evidence', [ed. R. Smith], *The Works of Jeremy Bentham*, ed. J. Bowring, 11 vols, Edinburgh, 1838-43, vol vi. 1-187. J. Bentham, *The Rationale of Judicial Evidence*, ed. J.S. Mill, 5 vols, London, 1827; Bowring, vi. 189-end & vii. *The Collected Works of Jeremy Bentham* are edited for The Bentham Committee and published by Oxford University Press; fourteen volumes, including eight of Correspondence, have appeared to date.

   A good account of Bentham's theory of evidence is contained in W. Twining, *Theories of Evidence: Bentham and Wigmore*, London, 1985, 19-108.

2   *In re an Inquiry under the Company Securities (Insider Dealing) Act 1985* [1988] 2 WLR 33 (CA and HL); [1988] 1 All ER 203 (HL).

the meaning of section 178(2) of the Act, namely 'the public interest in the protection of [journalists'] sources'.[4] Such an interest had already been recognised in section 10 of the Contempt of Court Act 1981 and in the *Guardian* case.[3]

Hoffmann's judgment was overturned in the Court of Appeal and this was affirmed by the House of Lords and the matter referred back to the Chancery Division, where Warner was eventually fined £20,000 for what the Vice-Chancellor referred to as 'a very serious contempt'.[4]

Bentham's Position on Disclosure of Sources

Bentham's principal position regarding the law of evidence can be summed up as 'Reveal everything that should not be excluded', coupled with a detailed examination of the proper grounds for exclusion. Proper exclusions, in Bentham's opinion, fall to be considered in the light of three criteria: vexation, delay and expense. The principle to be employed in weighing whether to require evidence to be given or not is to reckon the preponderant vexation, delay and expense of excluding it. In this, Bentham is addressing the legislator: it is not his intention that this weighing should be done by the jury, much less the judge, on every occasion of evidence being taken. Rather the legislator, guided by Bentham's detailed working out of the implications of the weighing, will arrive at a set of Cautionary Instructions, a sort of Code of Practice, which will guide judges in decision making. A first draft of such a set of Cautionary Instructions is printed in the Bowring edition as Appendix A to *An Introductory View*.[5] We are therefore, for Bentham, dealing with the very basic principles which inform the operation of the legal system. It is our conception of the system as a whole which is to be examined in the light of Bentham's theory, not the particular working out of individually litigated examples. Nothing could be further from Bentham's enterprise than the piecemeal attempts at reform in detail.[6]

In considering the principles of exclusion, Bentham first sets aside those cases in which no evidence need be produced at all, either because no good

---

3   Hoffmann J's judgment is quoted in part in [1988] 2 WLR at 46; *Secretary of State for Defence v Guardian Newspapers* [1985] AC 339. Mr Warner's replies to the Inspectors seem to have undergone editing before appearing in the official transcript, cf. [1988] 2 WLR at 39F.

4   [1988] 2 WLR 33; [1988] 1 All ER 203.

5   Bowring, vi, at 151 to 175.

6   As J.S. Mill observed in the preface to his edition of the *Rationale of Judicial Evidence* (Bowring, vi, at 202): 'The truth is, that bad as the English system of jurisprudence is, its parts harmonise tolerably well together: and if one part, however bad, be taken away, while another part is left standing, the arrangement which is substituted for it may, for a time, do more harm by its improper adaptation to the remainder of the old system, than the removing of the abuse can do good.'

would be served by the litigation it was designed to support (the litigation was abusive or frivolous), or because the litigation in question could be maintained without recourse to the particular evidence excluded, (that is, the plaintiff was able to establish his case satisfactorily without calling it or the defendant able adequately to defend himself without it). In showing this, Bentham demonstrates his awareness that the very production of evidence, in any circumstances, unavoidably discommodes somebody. It is always necessary, therefore, to justify the need to produce, to cause that degree of inconvenience necessary to produce it: only then, when one has reached as it were the threshold of the question, can one proceed to weigh the reasons for exclusion against inclusion. Once it has been established that the evidence is relevant and not unnecessary, however, it must be asked whether any *collateral* vexation, delay or expense will be produced by requiring its production. If so, it must be agreed whether the preponderant vexation lies with inclusion or exclusion, or whether insisting on the production of the evidence will cause greater inconvenience to those required to give it or to other interested parties than requiring its exclusion will cause to the party requiring its production.

The best way of grasping what Bentham is at here is by example of what he considers should be proper grounds for exclusion based on one or other of the heads of inconvenience: vexation, delay and expense. As regards witnesses, there is the vexation of travel to court, waiting in attendance at the court and returning home again. Again, in giving evidence the witness may be required to reveal matters which he or she would rather for personal reasons were not disclosed, or he or she may reveal secrets which interested others (including government) might wish to save from disclosure. On the one hand, Bentham notes that the witness ought not to be required to reveal everything (as an example of personal vexation he cites the case of the Chevalier d'Eon, concerning whose sex there was much contemporary debate in London society and about which a wager was laid: the wager being litigated, the Chevalier d'Eon was called to King's Bench as a witness).[7] On the other hand witnesses cannot be permitted the liberty of deciding for themselves when to keep silent. It is in this precise area that the question over journalists' privilege falls to be decided: does the preponderant vexation occasioned by the inclusion of the evidence – and consequent requirement that witnesses reveal what they know – outweigh the disadvantage to the witness (or some other interested party or parties) in requiring revelation of the evidence?

Before proceeding further with this distinct issue, however, I will for completeness' sake briefly sketch what Bentham has in mind when he speaks of the other inconveniences of delay and expense. Expense includes the cost in monetary terms of the production of the evidence and is, as Bentham himself acknowledges, merely one particular aspect of collateral vexation. Evidence

---

7   *Rationale of Judicial Evidence*, Bowring, vii, at 348n. The case, *Hayes v Jacques*, was tried before Lord Mansfield, the jury finding, wrongly as it subsequently proved, that the Chevalier was a woman: *Gentleman's Magazine*, xlvii, at 346.

should be excluded where the cost of its provision would fall on a third party not concerned in the lawsuit or where, even if it were to fall on one of the parties, its amount would be disproportionate to the expected gain from success in the litigation.

On the ground of delay, evidence should be excluded the production of which requires so much time that awaiting it causes more injustice than excluding it. If the evidence is indispensable to one or the other side then exclusion will rarely be the lesser injustice, unless there is a manifest vexation to the defendant, for example, in keeping him in prison pending trial of the issue.

To return now to cases of exclusion on the grounds of vexation. Bentham does not directly concern himself with the position of newspaper correspondents as witnesses, doubtless for the reasons cited in Philip Schofield's essay later in this collection,[8] because there was no distinct profession of journalism in Bentham's day and the issue which we face had not clearly manifested itself in this context. Bentham does, however, discuss in detail two examples which seem related, both to each other and to the present case. It appears to me possible to construct out of Bentham's treatment of these two concrete cases sufficient general principles to enable us to construct his views on the issue of journalists' privilege and so see what his view of The *Independent* case would have been.

Bentham's two examples are the Catholic priest in respect of confession and the lawyer with regard to his clients' communications. Bentham thinks that evidence of the first requested in connection with the prosecution of the confessor for a criminal act, which has been confessed to the priest, should be excluded, whereas the lawyer should, on the contrary, be required to reveal what his client has told him in confidence regarding the matter in dispute.[9]

More precisely, he argues as regards the Catholic priest, that he is neither compellable (that is, against his will) nor receivable (should he be anxious rather to give evidence). This view is perhaps the more remarkable in that Bentham was himself a professed atheist; though to be sure this in turn saved him from the anti-Catholic bias of the age. Catholic Emancipation was still some years off in 1813 when the bulk of his evidence writing was completed and it was still a felony to celebrate the Tridentine Mass. In the first place, Bentham argues that confession is so universal a practice amongst Roman Catholics that permitting the evidence of confession to be received would be a licence to plaintiffs and prosecutors to compel priests to give evidence upon all occasions when Roman Catholics were defendants and this would amount

---

8 Schofield, 'Bentham on Public Opinion and the Press' at p. 93 below.
9 *An Introductory View*, Bowring, vi, at 98 to 100. As in Bentham's day, English Law at present excludes the latter but admits, indeed compels the admission of, the former: *Wilson v Rastall* (1792) 4 Term Rep. 753; *Wheeler v Le Marchant* (1891) 17 Ch. D 675. As noted by Hoffmann J in this very case, the privilege of the legal profession is expressly saved by section 177(7) of the Financial Services Act 1986: see [1988] 2 WLR at 45H.

to an unjustifiable persecution of the Catholic religion. Furthermore, and perhaps more relevantly, such a provision would – by extirpating the practice of confession – produce more vexation than it would assuage, since the practice of confession is, in Bentham's view, otherwise extremely beneficial. The need to confess is both a deterrent upon the mind of the would-be transgressor and has also a reformative influence in case of actual transgression. Furthermore the penitential discipline exercised by the priest may well include the necessity of compensating victims for the harm occasioned by the wrongdoing. Bentham concludes by considering the only counterargument of importance, namely that the apparent *carte blanche* offered to penitents might stimulate the commission of crimes, only to dismiss the possibility: 'crimes of sectarian fanaticism apart, by this time nearly if not altogether out of date.'[10]

So far I have been relating Bentham's treatment of the subject in *An Introductory View*. In *The Rationale of Judicial Evidence* he adds[11] that the confessor may, without breaching the secret of the confessional, be in a position to convey useful preventive information to those threatened by a would-be penitent. Suppression of the practice of confession by too readily admitting the testimony would therefore remove a slight but additional safeguard from future victims. This point, coming after repetition of the wider, more political and philosophical considerations taken from *An Introductory View*, neatly exemplifies Bentham's penchant for the bathetic and banal, or to express it more charitably, the intensely pragmatic tendencies of his thought.

It is Bentham himself who links the exclusion of confession with the advisability of admitting clients' communications to their lawyers. He clearly revels in the outrage which he correctly expects such a suggestion will cause amongst the members of the legal profession:

'Call upon a man – of all men, call upon a man of law – to break his trust?' cries the man of law. Yes, surely, and why? Because the same reasons – the same considerations – of general utility and justice which in other cases call upon the minister of justice to compel the observance of a trust, call upon him in this case to compel the breach of it.[12]

The argument proceeds: 'a *trust* is but a species of *contract*' and 'mischievous contracts ought not to be formed.'

Note, that the same sinister interest, which, for the benefit of his own trade, engaged the man of law to secure to himself so convenient an exemption, engaged him, by means of the same uncontrolled power, to secure to himself the monopoly of it.[13]

---

10   *An Introductory View*, Bowring, vi, at 99.
11   Bowring, vii, at 366 to 368.
12   From the original manuscript preserved in Box xlv of the Bentham Manuscripts at University College London fol.238 (UC xlv, at 238). Cf. Bowring, vi, at 100n.
13   UC xlv, at 239 to 241. Cf. Bowring, vi, at 101n.

As Bentham proceeds to point out, the doctor who assists a malefactor is not protected from the need to betray his trust nor yet the banker.

What then are the arguments for permitting and requiring the lawyer to reveal his clients' communications? When someone is exempted from giving evidence against another, it may be for his own or for the other's benefit. 'Is it that the client would suffer so much more from being hurt by his lawyer's testimony than his own? or that a man is so much dearer to his advocate and his attorney than to himself?'[14] Bentham has already established to his own satisfaction that there is no objection to the receipt of self-incriminating evidence from the client himself. Indeed he supports positive public interrogation of defendants for the purpose of revealing information of which the defendant may be the only source.[15] It follows naturally that there can be, for him, no point in restraining the lawyer from revealing what can properly be asked of the client.

What advantage would accrue from compelling such evidence? The punishment of the guilty – 'to these and these alone, the man of law himself excepted, can an exemption of this sort be of any use.'[16] The good produced by this consequence quite outweighs any consideration relating to the breach of confidence between client and counsel – a confidence which from one point of view is an immoral one having for its object the preservation of the client from the ill effects of his criminous behaviour.

What benefits might flow from the maintenance of the exemption? Bentham's discussion here is, as frequently, skewed polemically by the fact that English law did, and does, maintain this particular exemption. Will confidence cease to be reposed in lawyers? Maybe, but what if it is? If a client is indeed guilty then he must weigh the disadvantages of being without a counsel to those of confiding what counsel may be obliged to reveal – but in any case the proper and requisite outcome is that he be found guilty and punished accordingly. Bentham is frequently forthright about this in his Utilitarian way and can in my opinion be rightly charged with a lack of common sense (for which of course there is little Utilitarian justification). If on the other hand he is innocent, he has nothing to fear from the revelations his counsel is compelled to make about him. 'Whence all this dread of truth? Whence comes it that any one loves darkness better than light, except it be that his deeds are evil?'[17] Would the lawyer, if confided in the more readily because his confidence is protected, be of any influence on his client, deterring him by advice from future offences or reforming him by exhortation in respect of past ones? 'On the contrary . . . the part taken by a lawyer in the character of Counsel for the

---

14 *Rationale of Judicial Evidence*, Bowring, vii, at 473.
15 *An Introductory View*, Bowring, vi, at 106 to 109. *Rationale of Judicial Evidence*, Bowring, vii, at 441ff. See Lewis, 'Bentham and the Right to Silence', *The Bentham Newsletter*, XII (1988), at 37 to 42.
16 UC xlv, at 235. Cf. Bowring, vi, at 99.
17 Editorial note by J.S. Mill to *Rationale of Judicial Evidence*, Bowring, vii, at 479.

Defendant, is exactly the part which is taken by an accessary after the fact to that same felony . . .'[18] In other words, Bentham does not look to lawyers to provide moral counsel. The chief consideration, therefore, which motivates Bentham to defend the secrecy of the confessional and deny that of the lawyers' office is the extent to which it produces reformation and repentance in the heart of the defendant.

Bentham, in fact, attributes the existence of the actual exemption in favour of lawyers, with its tendency to protect the guilty from punishment, explicitly to the lawyer's sinister interest: 'Expect the lawyer to be serious in his endeavours to extirpate the breed of dishonest litigants! Expect the foxhunter first to be serious in his wishes to extirpate the breed of foxes.'[19]

A Utilitarian Approach to The Independent Case

Now what of Warner?

Warner had received information which revealed the guilt of certain persons, the conviction of whom was the object of the investigators. Should he be required to reveal the information with the result that the guilty will be properly punished or should he be permitted to remain silent (or indeed also excluded from giving evidence altogether) on the ground of proponderant vexation? The vexation in this case would be of the sort referred to by Bentham as collateral: that is, it would not involve direct vexation to the parties to this dispute but rather either between some of the parties to this dispute and others (as when Warner sought to extract similar information from other informers who might prove more circumspect in the light of the fate of his earlier ones were he to reveal them) or between significant other parties altogether (such as other journalists seeking quite other information in similar circumstances where their informants risked prosecution if identified).

What benefits would flow from removing the collateral vexation? Bearing in mind that it was the publication of Warner's articles that first alerted the Inspectors to the possibility that certain persons were acting illegally, one might suppose that similar investigations in the future by Warner himself and other journalists would lead to the uncovering of further illegal activities which could then be investigated by the authorities. Like the priest's, the journalist's privilege would result in future benefits not easily obtainable in other ways. Such a consideration seems to underlie Hoffmann J's judgment that public interest supported the protection of journalists' sources.[20]

Unlike the priest, however, it is not clear that the journalist's claim to privilege is supported by any parallel salutary influence upon his informant's

---

18   UC xlv, at 236. Cf. Bowring, vi, at 100.
19   *Rationale of Judicial Evidence*, Bowring, vii, at 476.
20   [1988] 2 WLR at 46H.

activity, past or future. It is possible that the occasional informant acts out of remorse, but it seems more realistic to assume that it is done for money or favour. As for the future it is at least likely that a desire to be of similar assistance to the media in the future might rather promote than hinder involvement in illegality. The journalist, like the lawyer, has an interest in the continued lawlessness of his informants. This is not to suggest, any more than Bentham did, that journalists and lawyers actually promote illegality, but they undoubtedly thrive on it. Bentham's requirement that lawyers be committed to the extirpation of dishonesty over the needs of their current clients is one that can be easily applied to journalists. Revealing their sources may indeed make their task harder in the future. But if that task be defined as punishing the guilty rather than as writing good stories, it is not clear that the better course is not to reveal the sources and let the law take its course.

In the end it proves difficult to estimate what Bentham's attitude towards journalists' privilege might be. In my original seminar paper I suggested, rather to the audience's surprise, that Bentham would place the journalist with the lawyer rather than with the priest. Undoubtedly Bentham was capable of naivety where issues of civil liberty were involved, as his attitude to the question of self-incrimination shows. Needless to say he did not have the complexities of the modern state apparatus to attend to, not even a regular police force. He tended to the view that bad men were bad and required no defending whilst evincing a touching simplicity in the system's, that is his Natural system's, ability to tell bad from good. In his Natural world perhaps he could have afforded to take a hard line with journalists who declined to reveal their sources. We should, however, beware of adopting his conclusions and applying them in the different world of the Technical system with which, for all his efforts, we still operate.

Bentham on Public Opinion and the Press

Philip Schofield

Public Opinion as the Foundation of Government

By the end of the eighteenth century it had become common for British political theorists to stress the importance of public opinion to the stability of government. David Hume, as early as 1742, had asserted:

as Force is always on the side of the governed, the governors have nothing to support them but opinion. It is therefore, on opinion only that government is founded . . .[1]

Edmund Burke, in a famous pamphlet published in 1770, noted that opinion, which depended 'entirely' upon the 'voice of the people', was 'the great support of the State'. The operation of force and regulation was merely instrumental: 'Nations are not primarily ruled by laws; less by violence', but rather by a knowledge of the people. Hence, 'The temper of the people amongst whom he presides ought therefore to be the first study of a Statesman'.[2] William Paley, in his influential *Principles of Moral and Political Philosophy* (published 1785), likewise argued that opinion was the foundation of government. The balance of physical strength in a state always lay with the governed, hence:

In what manner opinion thus prevails over strength, or how power, which naturally belongs to superior force, is maintained in opposition to it, in other words, by what motives the many are induced to submit to the few, becomes an inquiry which lies at the root of almost every political speculation.

Paley, like Burke, emphasised the need for rulers to listen to opinion, to judge and take account of the public mood, not so much in order to follow it, but rather to influence and lead it.[3] The general mass of the people in eighteenth-century Britain were often equated with the mob, and the fear of mob rule,

---

Philip Schofield is a Research Fellow at the Bentham Project, University College London

1 *David Hume: The Philosophical Works*, ed. T.H. Green and T.H. Grose, 4 vols., London, 1882, iii, at 110.

2 See 'Thoughts on the Cause of the Present Discontents', in *The Writings and Speeches of Edmund Burke*, vol. II, ed. P. Langford, Cambridge, 1981, at 252.

3 See 'The Principles of Moral and Political Philosophy', in *The Works of William Paley, DD*, London, 1825, at 299 to 301.

of anarchy, was never far from the minds of rulers – fears apparently justified by such events as the Wilkite disturbances of the 1760s, the Gordon Riots of 1780, and most significantly the French Revolution. Politicians often drew a distinction between respectable opinion and the wild notions of the mob – public opinion was regarded as synonymous with the opinion professed by the higher or propertied orders of society: Burke in 1796, for instance, commented that the British public amounted only to some 400,000 persons.[4]

Such an approach to public opinion could not be in greater contrast to that advocated by Jeremy Bentham in his later democratic writings.[5] Bentham, who seems to have been the first major political theorist to enter into a detailed analysis of the subject,[6] argued that public opinion, and its most effective organ the periodical press, was a force not to be feared, but trusted; not indeed to be restricted to narrow limits, but allotted a central role in the political process. He wanted every member of the state to be involved in political decisions – the people in general were not to be manipulated by politicians, but rather to be encouraged to keep a close watch on their rulers to prevent them from betraying the trust reposed in them.[7] Bentham developed his ideas in a series of essays written in 1822 on the subject of constitutional law. Two of these, 'Economy as applied to Office' and 'Constitutional Code Rationale', forming the earliest writings for his projected constitutional code, contain an exposition of the more general principles which underlie his theory of representative democracy.[8] Each includes a substantial discussion of the role of public opinion in government. When Bentham briefly abandoned his work on the code in August 1822, he turned to an essay entitled 'Securities against Misrule', which occupied him for much of the remainder of the year.[9]

---

4   See 'Three Letters on the proposals for peace with the Regicide Directory of France', in *The Works of the Right Hon. Edmund Burke*, 2 vols., London, 1834, ii, at 289.

5   For Bentham's development as a political democrat see J.H. Burns, 'Bentham and the French Revolution', *Transactions of the Royal Historical Society*, xvi, 1966, 95 to 114; Michael James, 'Bentham's Democratic Theory at the time of the French Revolution', *The Bentham Newsletter*, x, 1986, at 5 to 16; J.R. Dinwiddy, 'Bentham's Transition to Political Radicalism', '1809 – 10', *Journal of the History of Ideas*, xxxvi, 1975, at 683 to 700; Douglas Long, 'Censorial Jurisprudence and Political Radicalism: A Reconsideration of the Early Bentham', *The Bentham Newsletter*, xii, 1988, at 4 to 23.

6   This is the conclusion reached by P.A. Palmer, 'The concept of public opinion in political theory', in C. Wittke, ed., *Essays in History and Political Theory in honor of Charles Howard McIlwain*, Cambridge, Mass., 1936, at 230 to 257 (see especially at 243 to 246).

7   Bentham saw political office as a trust in the sense of its being a power to be exercised for the benefit of the whole number of the members of the political community.

8   Though some of the manuscripts from these essays were incorporated into Book I of *Constitutional Code* in *The Works of Jeremy Bentham*, ed. J. Bowring, 11 vols., Edinburgh, 1843 (see vol. ix), they are published for the first time as coherent works in *First Principles preparatory to Constitutional Code*, ed. Philip Schofield, Oxford, 1989, as part of the new edition of *The Collected Works of Jeremy Bentham* [hereafter (*CW*)].

9   Never published in Bentham's lifetime, a version of this essay appeared in the Bowring edition (see viii, at 555 – 600). Since this transcription contains many inaccuracies and infelicities, references are here made to the original manuscripts in University College London Library.

Bentham had been introduced to the young Ambassador from Tripoli, Hassuna d'Ghies, and stimulated by this new friendship composed 'Securities against Misrule' as part of a plan to introduce representative institutions and liberal principles of government into the Barbary states.[10] The work included a Charter containing the detailed provisions of reform which Bentham hoped the Pasha of Tripoli could be induced to sanction, but a long introduction, entitled 'Preliminary Explanations', discusses the nature of public opinion, and in particular the significance of the press.[11]

Bentham's Rationale for a Representative Democracy

The starting point for an analysis of public opinion and the press in Bentham's theory of representative democracy is what he regarded as the major problem of government, namely corruption or the influence of sinister interest. He set down three principles as the basis of his political theory.[12] He commenced with the greatest happiness principle: 'The right and proper end of government in every political community is the greatest happiness of all the individuals of which it is composed.' He immediately modified this statement on the assumption that the happiness of some would always conflict with the happiness of others: so, 'instead of saying the greatest happiness of all, it becomes necessary to say the greatest happiness of the greatest number'. The second principle was the rulers' object-indicating principle: 'The actual end of government is in every political community the greatest happiness of those, whether one or many, by whom the powers of government are exercised.' This position could be verified by a study of the actions of past rulers, or else by reference to the inherent self-preference of human nature. The ruler if left to himself could not but act according to the self-preference principle – he would pursue his own particular interest, his sinister interest, at the expense of the general interest, the right and proper interest. The discrepancy which thus existed between the right and proper end of government and the sinister and actual end of government had to be removed: this required a third principle which Bentham called the means-prescribing or junction-of-interests prescribing principle, whereby the particular interest of rulers was brought into accordance with the universal interest. To effect this junction of interests, any sinister interest to

---

10   For the background to this plan see L.J. Hume, 'Preparations for Civil War in Tripoli in the 1820s: Ali Karamanli, Hassuna D'Ghies and Jeremy Bentham', *Journal of African History*, xxi, 1980, at 311 to 322.

11   These writings arguably contain a more cogent statement of Bentham's theory than can be gleaned from his pamphlet *On the Liberty of the Press and Public Discussion*, London, 1821 (Bowring, ii, at 275 to 297), which was directed more specifically to the contemporary situation in Spain, where a liberal government had come into power in 1820.

12   For a detailed exposition see Ross Harrison, *Bentham*, London, 1983, chapters V, VII and VIII.

which the ruler was exposed, that is any desire he might feel to sacrifice the general interest to his own particular interest, had to be nullified: this would leave that part of his interest which coincided with the general interest as the only interest by which his conduct could be determined.[13]

The means by which this was to be achieved was the maximisation of aptitude: aptitude was increased in proportion as an agent or set of agents was more likely to act in a way which increased the greatest happiness. For maximising aptitude on the part of government functionaries, the arrangements devised by constitutional law were to be termed securities for appropriate official aptitude.[14] Bentham divided aptitude into three elements or branches, moral, intellectual and active, of which the crucial branch was moral aptitude:

> To invest the ruler or rulers in chief in the political state in question with appropriate moral aptitude, and that in the highest degree, is . . . to place them in such a situation as that while they have no prospect of being able to encrease each of them his own happiness by diminishing the happiness of the greatest number, they have each of them a prospect of giving encrease to his own happiness by giving encrease to the happiness of the greatest number . . .[15]

Bentham's definition of moral aptitude amounted to the junction or identification of interests.

How then was the maximisation of aptitude to be achieved? The problem, of course, which faced the constitutional draftsman was the fact that:

> the particular interest of the ruling class is in a state of natural and diametrical opposition to that of the whole people considered in the correspondent character of subjects.[16]

The opposition of interests was manifested in political corruption, or the sinister sacrifice, the preference given to a particular interest to the detriment of a more general interest, the promotion of the happiness of the few to the detriment of the happiness of the many. The solution lay in a system of representative democracy, where the legislature was genuinely responsive to the wishes of the people and thus would act to promote the universal interest. Bentham explained that the universal interest was the aggregate of all the individual interests in the community – the secret ballot allowed each individual to vote for the candidate he considered the most likely to promote his own self-interest – the candidate elected would be the one who most successfully appealed to the interests of the greatest number of individuals in his electoral district.[17] In the legislative body, he would genuinely seek to

---

13   *First Principles (CW)*, at 232 to 236.
14   *Ibid.*, at 9.
15   *Ibid.*, at 14.
16   *Ibid.*, at 16.
17   Bentham's advocacy of the secret ballot in order that each individual might vote according to his conception of his self-interest contrasts with John Stuart Mill's advocacy of the open ballot in order that the individual might vote according to his conception of the public interest: see 'Considerations on Representative Government' in *Essays on Politics and Society*, vol. II, ed. John M. Robson, Toronto, 1977 (*Collected Works of John Stuart Mill*, vol. xix), at 488 to 495.

promote the universal interest, for he knew that if his constituents came to believe he was not acting in their interests they would remove him from his office, or refuse to re-elect him at the next annual election, or even subject him to judicially-administered punishment. The legislature was subject to the people, while the administrative departments of government (the executive and judiciary) were subject to the legislature. The rulers, with their particular interests, were made subject to the people, whose aggregate interests composed the universal interest: rulers could only promote their own individual interests through the share they had in the universal interest.[18]

The identification of interests was in this way achieved, and a constitutional framework established in which moral aptitude could be secured. But within this general framework a variety of more specific securities for appropriate aptitude had to be instituted – the very point of the system of representative democracy was that it guaranteed the effectiveness of these arrangements. In 'Economy as applied to Office', Bentham discussed six such securities for moral aptitude,[19] four of which he termed direct, acting on the power of the functionary, and two of which he termed indirect, acting against the desire or will of the functionary, to perform the sinister sacrifice. This division was founded on his theory of motivation: for an agent to act, both the will to act and a belief in his power to accomplish the act must be present. The four securities which diminished the power of the functionary to act were the minimisation of his official power (though of course allowing him the power necessary to the performance of his proper function),[20] the minimisation of the public money at his disposal, the minimisation of his pay, and the exclusion of factitious dignity, of titles of honour (these last three reducing the means he might have to corrupt others). The two securities which lessened his desire to perform the sinister sacrifice were the maximisation of legal responsibility (he was made legally punishable for any misdeed he committed) and – most importantly in Bentham's eyes – the maximisation of moral responsibility, the application of the moral or popular sanction by means of the Public Opinion Tribunal.[21] Moral responsibility was an extra-legal security which relied on the force of public opinion for its effect – the acts of the functionary were to be given maximum publicity so that in the event of his committing a misdeed or neglecting to perform a duty he would stand open to censure and loss of reputation in the eyes of the people. If he was a member of the legislative body, for instance, he might lose his seat at the next election; if an official in the administrative department, then his superior might feel

---

18 *First Principles (CW)*, at 30 to 35, 135 to 136.
19 He also recommended several securities for intellectual and active aptitude: see *ibid.*, at 77 to 94.
20 Central to this was the concept of subordination, a hierarchy of functionaries each individually responsible to his superior for the performance of certain defined tasks: see *Constitutional Code*, vol. I, ed. F. Rosen and J.H. Burns, Oxford, 1983 *(CW)*.
21 *First Principles (CW)*, at 27 to 29.

obliged to dismiss him; or in cases of exceptional aggravation, the functionary might be handed over to the judicial department, face trial and on conviction be subjected to legal punishment. In this way publicity, and the opinion grounded on it, gave essential support to the legal securities provided by constitutional law; in return the procedures established by constitutional law enabled that opinion to operate in an unobstructed manner.

The Public Opinion Tribunal

What then did Bentham mean by the related concepts of moral responsibility, the moral or popular sanction, and the Public Opinion Tribunal, and how did he envisage they would operate as a security for moral aptitude, in other words as a security against misrule? As early as *An Introduction to the Principles of Morals and Legislation* (printed in 1780, published in 1789), Bentham had distinguished four sanctions, the physical, political, moral and religious sanctions, which the legislator could make use of. A sanction was a source of motives – by providing motives, the expectation of pleasures or pains, action could be influenced. In his later writings he rarely spoke of the physical sanction – the motives arising from 'the ordinary course of nature' without human or supernatural intervention – perhaps regarding it as self-evident. He came to regard the religious sanction as an instrument purely of misrule, of bad government.[22] The political sanction, or what Bentham termed more fully the political, including the legal, sanction, had its source in the commands of the judge, acting according to the will of the supreme ruling power in the state – legal responsibility was subjection to the force of this sanction. The moral sanction had its source in the opinion of significant individuals:

If [the pleasure or pain takes place or is expected] at the hands of such *chance* persons in the community, as the party in question may happen in the course of his life to have concerns with, according to each man's spontaneous disposition, and not according to any settled or concerted rule, it may be said to issue from the *moral* or *popular* sanction.[23]

Moral responsibility, then, came about as a result of 'subjection – effective subjection – to the power of the popular, or say moral, sanction, as applied by the Public Opinion Tribunal'. This was analogous to legal responsibility, which was a result of subjection to the power of the political, including the legal, sanction as applied by the legal judicatories of the state. The Public Opinion Tribunal therefore operated in an analogous way to a court of law – but it was no more than an analogy, for the Public Opinion Tribunal was not an actually existing body:

---

22   See for instance *ibid.*, at 29.
23   *An Introduction to the Principles of Morals and Legislation*, ed. J.H. Burns and H.L.A. Hart, London, 1970 (CW), at 34 to 37.

By the term *Public Opinion Tribunal*, understand a fictitious entity − a fictitious tribunal the existence of which is, by the help of analogy, feigned under the pressure of inevitable necessity for the purpose of discourse to designate the imaginary tribunal or judiciary by which the punishments and rewards of which the popular or moral sanction is composed are applied.[24]

Who then belonged to this fictitious entity, who were its members? In a word, potentially everyone: it was composed of those, whoever they were and wherever they were, who could and did take cognisance of the subject under consideration − 'the inhabitants not only of the territory of the political state in question, but of every other territory on the earth's surface'.[25] The whole number of the members of a political community who were not physically incapable of acting as such were to be considered as members of the Public Opinion Tribunal; those members who at any point in time took cognisance of a matter − whether by publication, writing, reading or speech − formed a standing committee of the Public Opinion Tribunal; and of this standing committee, there were so many sub-committees as there were aggregates of individuals who on any one occasion, in any one place, likewise took cognisance of the matter. Of these sub-committees, an author could be regarded as a presiding member, or president; and of these, a newspaper editor,

being the only one in constant activity is, as it were, among the Presidents of these same Presidents: King of these Kings; Lord of these Lords of the dominion of Liberty and independence.

To belong to the Public Opinion Tribunal one simply needed to form an opinion on the subject in question: the decision thus made by each member of the Public Opinion Tribunal Bentham termed his suffrage.[26]

The force exerted by the popular or moral sanction depended upon 'notification' − this involved making known both the decision pronounced by the Public Opinion Tribunal considered as an aggregate and the grounds on which the decision was made. Bentham admitted that this decision could never be definitively ascertained, but it could be presumed. The presumption was a matter for each individual: from the particular circumstances of the case, and from his knowledge of the interests and views of the other members, each individual formed a conclusion respecting the decision likely to be taken by the other members of the Public Opinion Tribunal. The rectitude of the decision was not a matter of certainty − it was only comparative − but the decision pronounced by a majority had greater probability of rectitude than that pronounced by any minority.[27] The decision of the majority, in other words,

---

24 *First Principles (CW)*, at 283. For an analysis of 'fictitious entities' in Bentham's thought see Harrison, *Bentham*, chapter III.
25 *First Principles (CW)*, at 57.
26 University College London Library, Bentham Papers, box xxiv, fos. 242 to 246 (Bowring, viii, at 565 to 566).
27 *First Principles (CW)*, at 57.

was more likely to be conducive to the greatest happiness and was therefore to be taken for that of the Public Opinion Tribunal as a whole. Bentham's explanation was again related to his theory of motivation. Conduct would always be determined by interest, that is the actor's conception of his interest. The opinion acted upon by each member of the Public Opinion Tribunal would therefore be determined by his own interest. Where there was disagreement on a certain question, the Public Opinion Tribunal would be divided into two groups – the majority group Bentham called the democratical section, and the minority group the aristocratical section:

The interest of the Democratical Section is that of the majority of the Members of which the whole Tribunal taken in the aggregate is composed: it is consequently the interest of the subject many: the opinion on which it *acts* will be that which is in the highest degree contributory to the greatest happiness of the greatest number . . .

In contrast, the interest of the aristocratical section was that of the majority of the members of what Bentham called 'the ruling and otherwise influential few' – the highest ruling functionaries in the state and their allies. The interest of this section, and therefore the opinion pronounced by it, would in most cases be 'in direct opposition' to that of the democratical section. This meant that in practice the democratical section would attach 'disrepute' to those actions which its members considered to be detrimental to the universal interest, and 'good repute' to those which they considered contributory to it: expressions of disapprobation would be made towards the former, of approbation towards the latter. On the other hand, the aristocratical section would attach 'good repute' to those actions which its members considered to be contributory to its own particular interest – and since 'in a great, not to say the greater, part of the whole field of legislation', its interest was diametrically opposed to the democratical, it would approve of actions which tended to be detrimental to the universal interest. So the opposition of interests between rulers and subjects was mirrored in an opposition of opinions, and once again it was the majority, constituting the universal interest, which was to hold sway: the Public Opinion Tribunal being no more than the opinions of the aggregate number of persons who took cognisance of the matter, the opinion acted upon by 'the Tribunal considered as a whole [will] be determined by the interest of the majority of those who act as Members'.[28]

The point about good repute, or public approval, was that it was the cause of respect. Respect was not only a source of pleasure in itself to the person who formed the object of it, but also the source of services, of good offices – the person to whom respect was paid could expect to receive favours at the hands of those by whom it was paid. In contrast, ill-repute, or public disapproval, was the cause of disrespect – not only a source of pain in itself, but also the source of disservices, or ill-offices. The rewards and punishments

---

28   *Ibid.*, at 68 to 70.

of the moral sanction were every bit as real as those of the other sanctions. The functionary who acted in such a way as to promote the general interest would be praised by the Public Opinion Tribunal and thereby earn the respect of the people; the services which individuals would then perform for his benefit were both his inducement and reward for acting in that way. In contrast the functionary who acted in such a way as to promote a sinister interest would find himself condemned by the Public Opinion Tribunal and thereby earn the disrespect of the people; the disservices which individuals would perform to his disadvantage were both a discouragement to and a punishment for his acting in that way.[29]

Newspapers and the Public Opinion Tribunal

We have seen who made up the membership of the Public Opinion Tribunal, and in what way its decision could be presumed and in what sense it might be regarded as correct. But in order for a decision to be made, a prerequisite was appropriate information. The production of a suffrage, the forming of an opinion, required a stock of facts relating to the action in question, while the substance of the opinion could be influenced by arguments respecting the tendency of the action with reference to the general interest.[30] Bringing to bear the force of the Public Opinion Tribunal was therefore a complex process – information had to be presented, suffrages had to be produced, and then the suffrages had to be made known, they had to be given publicity, and this in itself involved a series of operations: extraction, registration, multiplication and diffusion (that is finding out, writing down, printing and circulating the opinion in question).

For all these several operations, one and the same article presents itself as the effectual, and the only effectual, instrument. This instrument is no other than a *Newspaper* . . .

The newspaper editor made comments, or put forward 'motions', whereupon those members of the community who read the newspaper, or conversed with those that did, gave their suffrages. The suffrages could not of course be counted, so 'the number of them must in each case be left to inference and conjecture'. The newspaper was a far more efficient instrument than pamphlets or books simply because of its 'regularity and constancy of attention' – it took notice of incidents as they took place. Indeed, in a representative democracy, the function of the newspaper editor was second only in importance to that of the principal minister – the minister gave impulse 'to the machinery of the political sanction', the editor of a popular newspaper 'to that of the social [that is, moral] sanction'.[31]

---

29 *Ibid.*, at 301 to 303, 306 to 309; UC clx, fos. 72 to 73.
30 *First Principles (CW)*, at 288.
31 UC xxiv, fos. 296 to 298 (Bowring, viii, at 579). Bentham's recommendations for conducting a newspaper are at UC xxiv, fos. 299 to 304 (Bowring, viii, at 579 to 581).

As we have seen, Bentham attempted to explain the nature of moral responsibility and the functioning of the Public Opinion Tribunal by means of analogy with legal responsibility and a legal judicatory. He acknowledged that at first glance the Public Opinion Tribunal 'will be apt to present itself as nothing more than the offspring of imagination and language: – a purely fictitious and verbal entity'. But by taking the business of a newspaper as an example of a sub-committee of the Public Opinion Tribunal, and comparing its operations with those of a legal judicatory, which no one would deem to be fictitious, the Public Opinion Tribunal would be seen to possess 'the substance of reality'. Bentham enumerated the functions of a legal judicatory as follows:

(1) receiving claims and accusations;
(2) receiving oppositions and defences;
(3) receiving, compelling, collecting and storing evidence;
(4) receiving and hearing arguments;
(5) forming a judgment and a correspondent will, that is coming to a decision and resolving to act in consequence;
(6) giving expression to such judgment and will;
(7) giving impression to such expression;
(8) giving diffusion to such expression;
(9) giving execution and effect to such judgment and will.

A newspaper performed the same operations. (1) The receipt by the editor of an allegation of misconduct on the part of a functionary was the equivalent of the receipt of an accusation in a judicatory. (2) and (3) The receipt by the editor of information from correspondents, the need which the accused party would feel to make a reply to the accusation (either to confess to the act or to deny it, or to present circumstances in justification of it), the coming forward of further witnesses, and the keeping and filing of the newspapers by the purchasers, was the equivalent of receiving, compelling, collecting and storing evidence. This at the same time amounted to the receiving of a defence. (4) Along with the evidence would inevitably come argument – either bringing to view the probability or improbability of the alleged act or of any alleged justificatory circumstances, or the propriety or impropriety of the act. This was the equivalent of receiving arguments, while the function of hearing this mass of evidence and argument was left to the readers. (5) and (6) The editor would form a judgment of his own on the matter and give expression to it. Suppose the judgment was declared in favour of conviction, and condemned the accused party – this was an opinion that the party in question had committed a disreputable act: in consequence of the expression of this opinion the estimation in which the party was held by the other members of the Public Opinion Tribunal would be lowered, and they would thereby deprive him of their good offices, and even possibly expose him to ill-offices:

in such judgment is naturally at least, if not necessarily and virtually, included the declaration of a will, or say a desire, that such should be the result.

(7) and (8) In the course of business, by the very production of the newspaper, the editor gave impression and diffusion to the expression of his judgment and will. (9) Effect and execution was given to the judgment by the consequent ill-offices which the delinquent received at the hands of the members of the Public Opinion Tribunal.[32]

Government and The Press

It was obvious why functionaries should want to limit the force of the Public Opinion Tribunal – it was the only effective counterforce to their power, and thus to their endeavours to promote their own interest to the detriment of the general interest. Now because the press was the most important of the channels by which information could be conveyed to the members of the Public Opinion Tribunal, and the most important of the channels by which publicity could be given to their decisions, it was a particular target of rulers. Bentham analysed the means which rulers could use to diminish the amount or accuracy of information which could reach the public, and therefore diminish the effectiveness of the moral or popular sanction. He identified two policies: (1) the blockading system or obstructive policy, by which the flow of information was stopped, either in whole or in part; (2) the corruptive policy, by which the information received was made corrupt and delusive. The obstructive policy merely stopped, or subtracted, useful information, whereas the corruptive policy added false information for the purpose of deception. However the obstructive policy could produce deception as well as the corruptive: the information allowed to pass on could be partial, all that on one side of a question being suppressed, all that on the other, which it was hoped to serve, being allowed through. Bentham further divided the obstructive policy into two modes of restriction, the licensing system and the prosecuting system. Under the licensing system, prohibition was the essential element: in the first place, everything was prohibited; and in the next place, permission was granted to certain persons or things as the rulers thought fit. Under the prosecuting system, it was only after publication that prosecution before a legal judicatory could take place. The prosecuting system was thus much less efficient than the licensing system: firstly, the prosecuting system could only be employed when the very thing it aimed to prevent had actually been done – the paper had been published; secondly, its effect was comparatively uncertain: under the licensing system, a publisher could be certain that he

---

32   UC xxiv, fos. 236, 248 to 252 (Bowring, viii, at 564, 566 to 568).

would not be allowed to sell his publication, and therefore denied recompense; this would remove any motivation he might have to spend time, labour and money producing it in the first place; thirdly, prosecution was always attended with uncertainty, as well as delay, expense and vexation, on the side of the prosecutor; fourthly, the prosecution itself would attract attention, whereas licensing operated unobserved.

Thus [the licensing system] is not only so much more efficacious than punishment under the name of punishment, but at the same time less odious. It affords just ground for greater odium, yet attracts less. While it is less odious, it is beyond all comparison more mischievous.

Prohibition itself could again be divided into the case where it was complete – prohibition proper – or that where it was incomplete, as in the case of taxation. Payment of the tax was a licence to use the article; omission to pay the tax resulted in the refusal of the licence. The taxing system favoured the rich to the detriment of the poor:

That which the poor [man] has need of to enable him to form a right judgment and pursue a line of conduct beneficial to his interest is stopt from reaching him: while his comparatively rich antagonist receives the matter on both sides.

The rich were supplied with the means of attack, the poor deprived of the means of defence.[33] Bentham was writing at a time which has been described as 'the high-water mark of legislation restricting the freedom of the Press',[34] and as an example of the taxing system seems to have had in mind the stamp duty payable on newspapers, and its extension by the Newspaper Stamp Duties Act,[35] one of the so-called Six Acts of 1819, to pamphlets containing news and comment. This had effectively destroyed the cheap radical press. He felt that the taxing system was not so mischievous as prohibition proper and the prosecuting system – the control was not so rigorous – but it was still mischievous enough. Whatever form the restriction on the press took, there could be no doubt as to its end:

As it is only by the power of government that this corruption and this obstruction can be carried into effect, it is manifestly for the purpose of misrule, for the purpose of giving extension and perpetuity to misrule, and thereby to human misery in all its shapes, that war upon the happiness of mankind in both these shapes is on every occasion carried on.[36]

The ruler or rulers who attempted to obstruct or corrupt the flow of information, by that very act 'betray their intention to push to consummation the sinister sacrifice'; morever,

By no finite number of determinate acts of tyranny could a more proper and reasonable cause for resistance and insurrection be afforded, supposing success in a sufficient degree probable.

---

33 *First Principles (CW)*, at 292 to 295.
34 A. Aspinall, *Politics and the Press c. 1780-1850*, London, 1949, at 59.
35 60 Geo. III and 1 Geo. IV, c. 9.
36 *First Principles (CW)* at 295.

The conduct of a government could in all other respects be exemplary, yet if this one restraint existed, then the only supposition that 'a true lover of mankind' would require to make it desirable that the government should be destroyed, was that under the ensuing government this restraint would not be imposed.[37] It was, according to Bentham, highly unlikely that a representative democracy would attempt to impose such restrictions – they were much more likely to be found in other forms of government.[38]

Publicity Subordinate to Utility

However a qualification need be added. The structure of representative democracy was not an end in itself, but a means – albeit the only means – of securing appropriate moral aptitude, and thereby ensuring that government acted in the general interest, promoted the greatest happiness of the greatest number, and did not act in the self-interest of rulers, promoted the greatest happiness of a smaller number. In the same way, the security to convey and receive information was only a means and not an absolute right – such a security had always to be measured against the criterion of utility. Publicity was not to be accorded to acts where its effect would be to reduce, rather than to increase, the greatest happiness; where the evil was produced not by the act itself, but by the disclosure of it. For instance in certain areas of private morals, 'for want of sufficient maturity in the public judgment, or by the influence of some sinister interest', public opinion might condemn an act which on balance was not pernicious. Where a community was intolerant in matters of religion, the disclosure of an opinion contrary to the predominant one would fit this case; or where a community was hostile to homosexuality, the act itself produced no evil yet by its disclosure 'a whole life may be filled with misery'.[39] In *Constitutional Code* this principle was applied to matters which came into the field of national security, though it was always incumbent upon the functionary to justify the continuation of the secrecy, and not on the public to justify the release of the information.[40]

Conclusion

Bentham may be regarded as having been unduly optimistic in his emphasis on the efficacy of public opinion and the press in a representative democracy as

---

37 *Ibid.*, at 297 to 298.
38 Bentham did accept that defamation should be punishable at law when it was 'the result of wilful mendacity, accompanied with the consciousness of its falsity, or else with culpable rashness', but argued that the truth of the accusation should be a sufficient defence: *On the Liberty of the Press and Public Discussion*, at 12 (Bowring, ii, at 279).
39 *First Principles (CW)*, at 290.
40 *Constitutional Code*, vol. I (CW), at 166 to 168.

the means of promoting the greatest happiness. Nevertheless the increasing influence of public opinion was perhaps one of the most startling political developments of the reign of George III; moreover in the early nineteenth century, the press, emancipating itself from the control of politicians, began to take seriously its role as the Fourth Estate – and the papers which were most successful in terms of circulation, *The Times, Morning Chronicle*, and *The Courier*, were those most clearly perceived to be exercising editorial independence. Furthermore the view that an enlightened public was the major instrument of reform, that only ignorance prevented the people from abolishing tyranny, was a regular theme in radical political theory. Richard Price in 1789, for instance, had commented that the nations of the world were quiescent under despotism solely because of their want of knowledge:

Enlighten them and you will elevate them. . . . Give them just ideas of civil government, and let them know that it is an expedient for gaining protection against injury and defending their rights, and it will be impossible for them to submit to governments which, like most of those now in the world, are usurpations on the rights of men, and little better than contrivances for enabling the *few* to oppress the *many*.[41]

Thomas Paine, in *Rights of Man*, argued that the French Revolution was

no more than the consequence of a mental revolution previously existing in France. The mind of the nation had changed beforehand, and the new order of things had naturally followed the new order of thoughts.

This new order had been brought about by the writings of Montesquieu, Voltaire, Rousseau, Raynal, Quesnay and Turgot, and been given a practical manifestation in the principles of the American Revolution.[42] Perhaps Bentham did have cause to think there were close ties between a free press and the maintenance of the democratic state.

---

41   Richard Price, *A Discourse on the Love of our Country*, London, 1789, at 12.
42   Thomas Paine, *Rights of Man*, London, 1791, at 85 to 89.